# NEXT STEPS FOR ASEAN+3 CENTRAL SECURITIES DEPOSITORY AND REAL-TIME GROSS SETTLEMENT LINKAGES

A Progress Report of the Cross-Border Settlement Infrastructure Forum

JULY 2020

ADB

ASIAN DEVELOPMENT BANK

Corrigenda to ADB publications may be found at http://www.adb.org/publications/corrigenda.

Notes:
ADB recognizes "China" as the People's Republic of China; "Hong Kong" as Hong Kong, China; "Korea" as the Republic of Korea; and "Vietnam" as Viet Nam.

In this report, international standards for naming conventions—International Organization for Standardization (ISO) 3166 for country codes and ISO 4217 for currency codes—are used to reflect the discussions of the ASEAN+3 Bond Market Forum to promote and support implementation of international standards in financial transactions in the region. ASEAN+3 comprises the Association of Southeast Asian Nations (ASEAN) plus the People's Republic of China, Japan, and the Republic of Korea.

The economies of ASEAN+3 as defined in ISO 3166 include Brunei Darussalam (BN; BRN); Cambodia (KH; KHM); the People's Republic of China (CN; CHN); Hong Kong, China (HK; HKG); Indonesia (ID; IDN); Japan (JP; JPN); the Republic of Korea (KR; KOR); the Lao People's Democratic Republic (LA; LAO); Malaysia (MY; MYS); Myanmar (MM; MMR); the Philippines (PH; PHL); Singapore (SG; SGP); Thailand (TH; THA); and Viet Nam (VN; VNM). The currencies of ASEAN+3 as defined in ISO 4217 include the Brunei dollar (BND), Cambodian riel (KHR), Yuan Renminbi (CNY), Hong Kong dollar (HKD), Indonesian rupiah (IDR), Japanese yen (JPY), Korean won (KRW), Lao kip (LAK), Malaysian ringgit (MYR), Myanmar kyat (MMK), Philippine peso (PHP), Singapore dollar (SGD), Thai baht (THB), and Vietnamese dong (VND).

Printed on recycled paper

# CONTENTS

# TABLES AND FIGURES

# FOREWORD

The lack of well-developed local currency (LCY) bond markets is regarded as a cause of the maturity and currency mismatches—also known as the "double mismatch problem"—that negatively affected borrowers in the region during the 1997/98 Asian financial crisis. With that in mind, ASEAN+3 finance ministers established the Asian Bond Markets Initiative (ABMI) in 2002 to boost the development of LCY bond markets to help mitigate the double mismatch problem and recycle the vast amount of savings within the region to support needed infrastructure investments.[1]

As a way of promoting intraregional financial transactions under ABMI, the foundation of a regional settlement intermediary (RSI) was proposed. In 2013, the Cross-Border Settlement Infrastructure Forum (CSIF) was established by regional central banks and central securities depositories to consider RSI options. In 2014, after a series of studies and discussions, the CSIF chose central securities depository (CSD)–real-time gross settlement (RTGS) linkage as a model for the RSI. CSD–RTGS linkage is a bilateral linkage between two markets. By linking national CSD and central banks' RTGS systems in two markets, the model can realize cross-border delivery versus payment settlement to enable safe and efficient cross-border financial transactions.

This document explains the progress of ongoing CSIF discussions and explores the way forward. Establishing a sound and efficient RSI is an effective way to stimulate intraregional financial investment. CSIF's continued discussion will support the development of an RSI and promote financial integration within ASEAN+3.

Yasuyuki Sawada
Chief Economist and Director General
Economic Research and Regional Cooperation Department

---

[1] The Association of Southeast Asian Nations (ASEAN)+3 comprises the 10 members of ASEAN plus the People's Republic of China, Japan, and the Republic of Korea.

# ACKNOWLEDGMENTS

The Cross-Border Settlement Infrastructure Forum (CSIF) was established under the Asian Bond Markets Initiative after being endorsed in May 2013 in Delhi at the meeting of finance ministers and central bank governors from members of the Association of Southeast Asian Nations (ASEAN) as well as the People's Republic of China, Japan, and the Republic of Korea—a grouping that is collectively known as ASEAN+3. The chair and vice-chair of the CSIF have been leading discussions to implement a regional settlement intermediary (RSI), with the Asian Development Bank serving as the Secretariat. CSIF members have contributed to discussions by sharing information on the status of their respective financial market infrastructure, in particular the real-time gross settlement (RTGS) and central securities depository (CSD) systems in each of their economies.

This report shares the outcomes of regional discussions on and progress made toward establishing an efficient and effective RSI. It is the crystallization of the region's shared knowledge and collaborative efforts toward more harmonized and integrated ASEAN+3 bond markets that has resulted from the strong support and cooperation of the region's central banks, CSDs, and authorities participating as observers, as well as experts from other regions.

Members of the CSIF Secretariat—led by Satoru (Tomo) Yamadera and including Kosintr Puongsophol, Byung-Wook Ahn, and Yvonne Osonia, as well as Asian Development Bank consultants, Jae-Hyun Choi and Taiji Inui—express their heartfelt gratitude to CSIF members and observers. The CSIF Secretariat also would like to thank the CSIF chair and vice-chair for guiding all discussions toward fruitful results.

No part of the report represents the official views of any of the institutions that participated as CSIF members or observers. The CSIF Secretariat bears sole responsibility for the contents of this report.

# ABBREVIATIONS

| | |
|---|---|
| ABMI | Asian Bond Markets Initiative |
| ASEAN | Association of Southeast Asian Nations |
| BCP | business continuity planning |
| BIC | Business Identifier Code |
| CMU | Central Moneymarkets Unit |
| CSD | central securities depository |
| CSIF | Cross-Border Settlement Infrastructure Forum |
| DLT | distributed ledger technology |
| DVP | delivery versus payment |
| FMI | financial market infrastructure |
| HKMA | Hong Kong Monetary Authority |
| HQLA | high-quality liquid assets |
| HVPS | high-value payment system |
| ISIN | International Securities Identification Number |
| ISO | International Organization for Standardization |
| LCY | local currency |
| Lao PDR | Lao People's Democratic Republic |
| PRC | People's Republic of China |
| PSMS | Pre-Settlement Matching System |
| PVP | payment versus payment |
| RSI | regional settlement intermediary |
| RTGS | real-time gross settlement |
| repo | repurchase agreement |
| TARGET | Trans-European Automated Real-Time Gross Settlement Express Transfer System |
| TF4 | Task Force 4 |
| US | United States |

# STATEMENT FROM THE CSIF CHAIRS

The chair and vice-chair express their heartfelt gratitude to the members and observers of the Cross-Border Settlement Infrastructure Forum (CSIF) for their contributions to this initiative. The chair and vice-chair look forward to the continuous support of members and observers. The chairs also greatly appreciate the support of the Asian Development Bank Secretariat, including the consultants who helped draft this report.

Soulysak Thamnuvong
Chair of the CSIF
Director General, Payment Systems Department
Bank of the Lao PDR

Seung-Kwon Lee
Vice-Chair of the CSIF
Director, Global Business Department
Korea Securities Depository

# EXECUTIVE SUMMARY

The Cross-Border Settlement Infrastructure Forum (CSIF) was established under the Asian Bond Markets Initiative (ABMI) after being endorsed in May 2013 in Delhi at the meeting of finance ministers and central bank governors of the Association of Southeast Asian Nations (ASEAN), the People's Republic of China, Japan, and the Republic of Korea—a grouping that is collectively known as ASEAN+3.

ABMI has conducted several studies on establishing a regional settlement intermediary (RSI). Based on the findings, the CSIF has proposed central securities depository (CSD)–real-time gross settlement (RTGS) linkage as the best model to establish an RSI. CSD–RTGS linkage can be categorized into three types: (i) cross-border delivery versus payment (DVP), (ii) CSD–CSD linkage, and (iii) RTGS–RTGS linkage for payment versus payment. The following are the models of the three types implemented or to be implemented in the region:

(i)     the first category shall rely on the cross-border DVP being developed by the Bank of Japan  and the Hong Kong Monetary Authority (HKMA) with the Bank of Japan Financial Network System Japanese Government Bond Services and the Clearing House Automated Transfer System, targeted to be launched in spring 2021;

(ii)    the model for the second category is that of the China Central Depository & Clearing Co. Ltd. and Korea Securities Depository implemented in 2017 based on a desktop study conducted then; and

(iii)   the model for the third category is that of the HKMA and Hong Kong Interbank Clearing Limited connecting domestic and some cross-border RTGS systems (operating for years, as mentioned in the report).

To take advantage of these accomplishments and initiatives, the CSIF may pursue moving toward centralized integration based on such models that would lead to more bilateral agreements.

Also, as a sign of growing regional cooperation under ABMI, all CSIF members will adopt international standards, including ISO 20022 (possibly by 2023), as the basis for cross-border transactions. Further, amid the current regulatory trend of collateralization in cross-border transactions, the CSIF discussed freeing up the region's domestic collateral pools for use in cross-border transactions.

The CSIF will also need to consider the implications of recent advancements in financial technology. Distributed ledger technology and blockchain will soon be employed as part of payment and settlement infrastructure in the region. Given these rapid developments, it is necessary to take stock of the varied experiences of CSIF members.

# I.   INTRODUCTION

The Asian Bond Markets Initiative (ABMI) has conducted several studies on establishing a regional settlement intermediary (RSI). The development of efficient and sound market infrastructure for regional securities settlement is regarded as one of the key components of ABMI. The Group of Experts published a report in April 2010 that analyzed possible RSI models from the viewpoint of legal and business feasibility. After the Group of Experts report, a series of reassessments were made and the establishment of a Cross-Border Settlement Infrastructure Forum (CSIF) was endorsed at the 2013 meeting in Delhi of finance ministers and central bank governors from members of the Association of Southeast Asian Nations (ASEAN) plus the People's Republic of China, Japan, and the Republic of Korea (ASEAN+3). The discussions at this meeting focused on the improvement of cross-border bond and cash settlement infrastructure in the region, including the possibility of establishing an RSI.

The CSIF consists of the central banks and national central securities depositories (CSDs) of ASEAN+3 members, with market regulators and officials from the region's ministries of finance joining as observers (Appendix 1). The CSIF reports to ABMI Task Force 4 (TF4) at least twice a year (Figure 1).

The CSIF aims to

(i)     enhance dialogue among policy makers and operators of bond and cash settlement infrastructure in the region;

(ii)    assess existing settlement infrastructure and identify comprehensive issues and requirements to facilitate cross-border bond and cash settlement infrastructure in the region;

(iii)   develop common basic principles for cross-border bond and cash settlement infrastructure with medium- and long-term perspectives; and

(iv)   discuss prospective models, an overall roadmap, and an implementation plan for establishment of cross-border bond and cash settlement infrastructure in the region.

**Figure 1: Structure of the Cross-Border Settlement Infrastructure Forum**

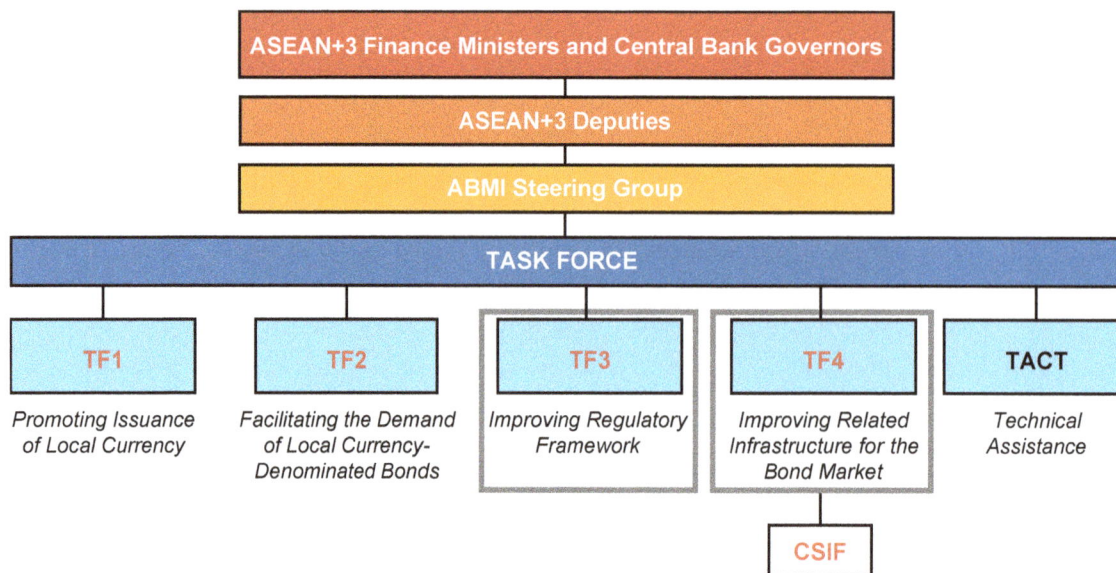

| | | | | |
|---|---|---|---|---|
| | | **ASEAN+3 Finance Ministers and Central Bank Governors** | | |
| | | **ASEAN+3 Deputies** | | |
| | | **ABMI Steering Group** | | |
| | | **TASK FORCE** | | |
| **TF1** | **TF2** | **TF3** | **TF4** | **TACT** |
| *Promoting Issuance of Local Currency* | *Facilitating the Demand of Local Currency-Denominated Bonds* | *Improving Regulatory Framework* | *Improving Related Infrastructure for the Bond Market* | *Technical Assistance* |
| | | | **CSIF** | |

ABMI = Asian Bond Markets Initiative; ASEAN+3 = Association of Southeast Asian Nations plus the People's Republic of China; Japan; and the Republic of Korea; CSIF = Cross-Border Settlement Infrastructure Forum; TACT = technical assistance and coordination team; TF = task force.

Source: Authors' illustration based on Asian Development Bank. 2019. *Good Practices for Developing a Local Currency Bond Market*. Manila.

Since its inception, the CSIF has submitted the following reports to ABMI TF4, which have been published upon approval by the ASEAN+3 finance and central bank deputies and endorsement by the ASEAN+3 finance ministers and central bank governors:

(i)     Basic Principles on Establishing a Regional Settlement Intermediary and Next Steps Forward (May 2014);

(ii)    Progress Report on Establishing a Regional Settlement Intermediary and Next Steps: Implementing Central Securities Depository–Real-Time Gross Settlement Linkages in ASEAN+3 (May 2015);

(iii)   Common Understanding on Cross-Border Business Continuity Planning and Cybersecurity (May 2018); and

(iv)    Common Understanding on International Standards and Gateways for Central Securities Depository and Real-Time Gross Settlement Linkages (May 2019).

This report details the progress of the CSIF discussions and possible next steps. Given the rapid pace of change, it may be necessary to review and reconsider what kind of technological options are best suited to the region.

# II. SALIENT POINTS IN PREVIOUS REPORTS

## A. Basic Principles on Establishing a Regional Settlement Intermediary and Next Steps Forward

In *Basic Principles on Establishing a Regional Settlement Intermediary and Next Steps Forward*, the CSIF proposed CSD–RTGS linkages as the best bilateral model to ensure the safety of settlement-connecting financial market infrastructures (FMIs) in ASEAN+3. Furthermore, CSD–RTGS linkages are compliant with international standards for enhancing the interoperability of FMIs (Figure 2).

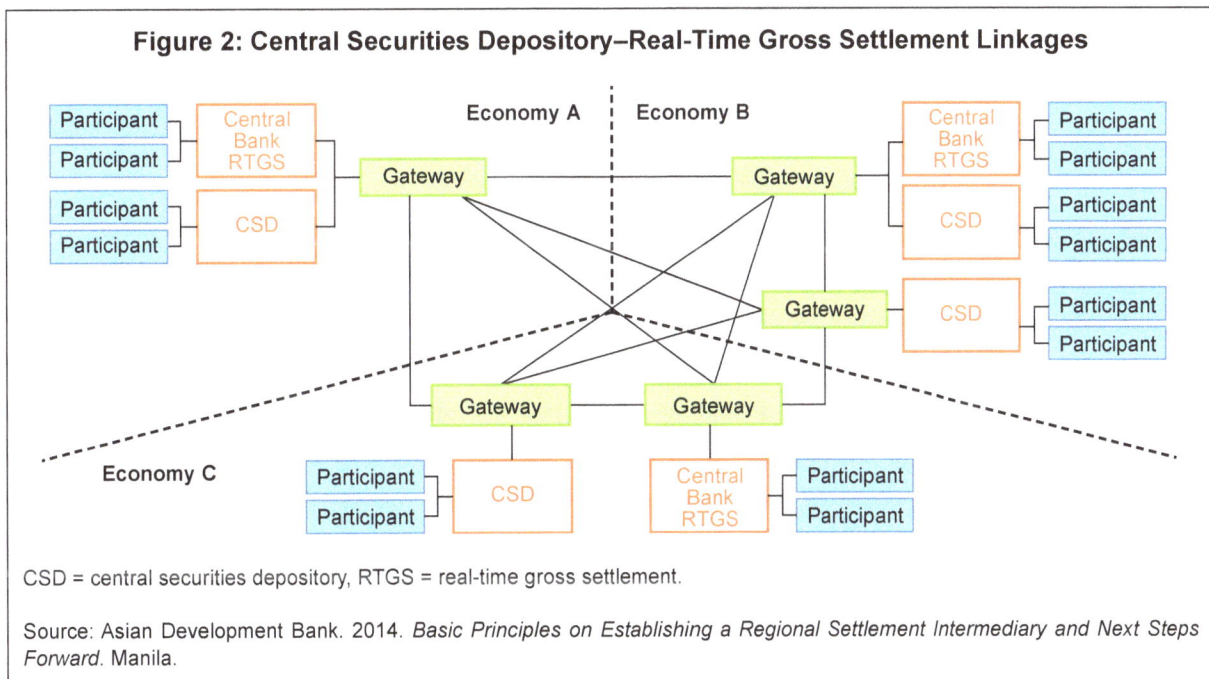

**Figure 2: Central Securities Depository–Real-Time Gross Settlement Linkages**

CSD = central securities depository, RTGS = real-time gross settlement.

Source: Asian Development Bank. 2014. *Basic Principles on Establishing a Regional Settlement Intermediary and Next Steps Forward*. Manila.

To choose the best RSI option, the CSIF identified the following basic principles in planning and designing an RSI for the region:

Principle 1:  Domesticity and cost efficiency: Maximize utilization of existing cash and bond settlement infrastructure.

Principle 2:  Safety: As recommended in the "Principles for Financial Market Infrastructures," cash settlement should use central bank money where practical and available.

Principle 3:  Flexibility: Allow newcomers to join when the market is reasonably developed and ready.

Principle 4:  Accessibility: Structure that small and medium-sized local financial institutions can benefit (not just for major and global players).

Principle 5:  Gradual integration: Start from bilateral links. Explore the possibility of centralized integration as long-term goal.

Principle 6:  Consistency and collaboration with other initiatives: Explore greater benefit by maintaining consistency and collaboration with other initiatives of the region.

Principle 7:  Standardization: Standardize market practices and technical aspects among members as much as possible to minimize costs.

Principle 8:  Harmonization of rules and regulations: Harmonize rules and regulations, as much as practical, that hinder cross-border transaction, including those that require holistic policy considerations such as capital controls and taxation, among others.

## B.   Progress Report on Establishing a Regional Settlement Intermediary and Next Steps: Implementing Central Securities Depository–Real-Time Gross Settlement Linkages in ASEAN+3

The *Progress Report on Establishing a Regional Settlement Intermediary and Next Steps: Implementing Central Securities Depository–Real-Time Gross Settlement Linkages in ASEAN+3*, published in 2015, described three types of CSD–RTGS linkages: (i) cross-border delivery versus payment (DVP), (ii) CSD–CSD linkage, and (iii) payment versus payment (PVP) (Figure 3).

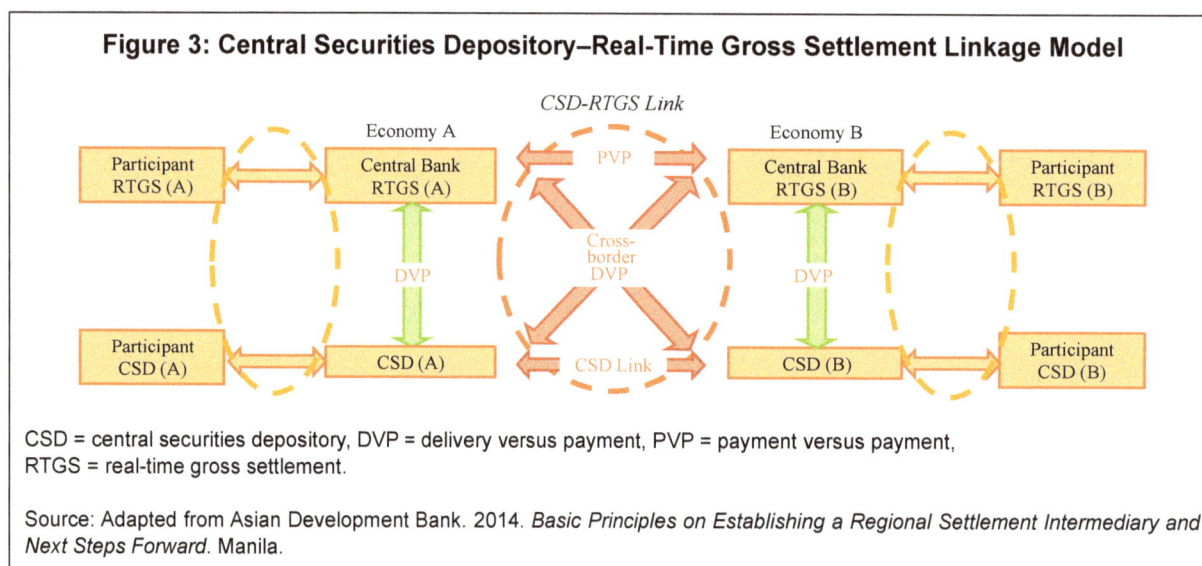

**Figure 3: Central Securities Depository–Real-Time Gross Settlement Linkage Model**

CSD = central securities depository, DVP = delivery versus payment, PVP = payment versus payment, RTGS = real-time gross settlement.

Source: Adapted from Asian Development Bank. 2014. *Basic Principles on Establishing a Regional Settlement Intermediary and Next Steps Forward*. Manila.

Cross-border DVP connects an RTGS system for cash settlement and a CSD system for securities settlement located in different economies to guarantee the settlement of both cash and securities completely. In other words, delivery of securities occurs if only if the correspondent payment (cash settlement) occurs.

A CSD–CSD linkage connects CSD systems located in two different economies, which enables to buy and sell securities in one economy from other economy.

PVP linkage connects RTGS systems located in different economies. PVP is a settlement mechanism that ensures that the final transfer of a payment in one currency occurs only if the final transfer of a payment in another currency or currencies takes place.

In the aforementioned report, the CSIF set out a roadmap for establishing CSD–RTGS linkages in ASEAN+3 (Figure 4).

CSIF members also discussed (i) fit and gap analysis of cross-currency DVP, (ii) possible implications of CSD–RTGS linkages, and (iii) policy recommendations and next steps. Regarding the fit and gap analysis, further study has been made, the outcome of which was shared at subsequent CSIF meetings.

## C.    Common Understanding on Cross-Border Business Continuity Planning and Cybersecurity

*Common Understanding on Cross-Border Business Continuity Planning and Cybersecurity* was published to establish a basic framework of cross-border business continuity planning (BCP) and cybersecurity, focusing on cross-border CSD–RTGS linkages. The CSIF recognized that all participants in CSD–RTGS linkages must have the same level of safety and soundness in their infrastructure. When connecting CSD and RTGS systems, the security measures of counterparty market infrastructure (CSD or RTGS system) are critical. As a prerequisite, CSD and RTGS systems must ensure sufficient levels of security to be connected with other CSD and RTGS systems through the linkages. Otherwise, the network will be vulnerable. The report discussed five key elements necessary to establish sound and resilient cross-border payment and settlement systems within the region: (i) governance, (ii) compliance, (iii) relevance, (iv) understanding, and (v) identification.

# Figure 4: Roadmap for Establishing a Regional Settlement Intermediary in ASEAN+3

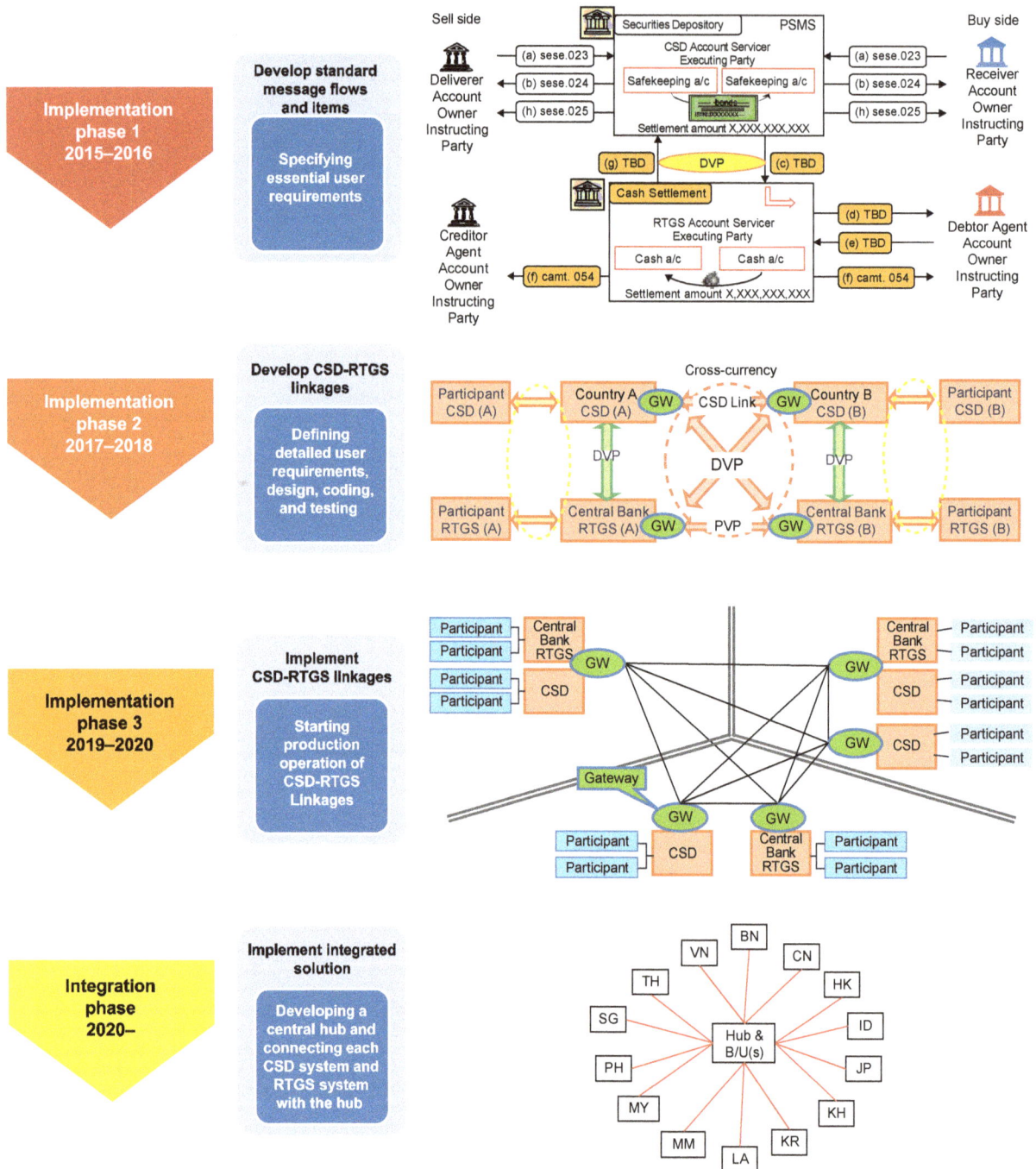

ASEAN+3 = Association of Southeast Asian Nations plus the People's Republic of China, Japan, and the Republic of Korea; BN = Brunei Darussalam; B/U = backup; CN = People's Republic of China; CSD = central securities depository; DVP = delivery versus payment; GW = gateway; HK = Hong Kong, China; ID = Indonesia; JP = Japan; KH = Cambodia; KR = Republic of Korea; LA = Lao People's Democratic Republic; MM = Myanmar; MY = Malaysia; PH = Philippines; PSMS = Pre-Settlement Matching System; PVP = payment versus payment; RTGS = real-time gross settlement; SG = Singapore; TBD = to be determined; TH =Thailand; VN = Viet Nam.

Source: Asian Development Bank. 2015. *Progress Report on Establishing a Regional Settlement Intermediary and Next Steps*. Manila.

Ideally, this set of common elements should be reviewed and updated from time to time. When establishing linkages among CSIF members, it is necessary to either consider a framework of mutual assurance or recognize the security framework of counterparty market infrastructure operators. In each economy, operators of CSD and RTGS systems, as well as the financial authorities, oversee and examine participants in their payment and settlement network. As the operators and financial authorities, they can set standards and check the level of security of each network participant. In the case of CSD–RTGS linkages, there is no central authority that can oversee the CSD and RTGS system operators of participating markets. Therefore, when connecting CSD and RTGS systems bilaterally, market infrastructure operators of both sides of the transaction need to disclose and exchange necessary information. In addition, they may need to check each other's level of security to ensure the safety and soundness of all systems when establishing linkages.[1]

## D. Common Understanding on International Standards and Gateways for Central Securities Depository and Real-Time Gross Settlement Linkages

*Common Understanding on International Standards and Gateways for Central Securities Depository and Real-Time Gross Settlement Linkages* consists of two parts: (i) creating a common understanding among CSIF members on international standards for those linkages, and (ii) establishing general user requirements and technical specifications for linkage gateways.

### 1. International standards to be used for CSD–RTGS linkages

International standards to be used for CSD–RTGS linkages include

(i) International Organization for Standardization (ISO) 20022 for messages,

(ii) ISO 3166 for country codes,

(iii) ISO 4217 for currency codes,

(iv) ISO 6166 (International Securities Identification Number [ISIN]) for securities numbering,

(v) ISO 9362 (Business Identifier Code [BIC]) for financial institution identification, and

(vi) ISO 8601 for date and time.

---

[1] Common Criteria for Information Technology Security Evaluation, which follows ISO/IEC 15408, is the basis for the evaluation of security properties of information technology products.

Descriptions of these individual standards are provided below.

(i)    ISO 20022 for messages

Upon discussing the key ISO 20022 messages, the following basic concepts may be adopted to make implementation easier:

(a)    Mandatory items in ISO 20022 message definition reports are also to be mandatory for CSD–RTGS linkage messages.

(b)    Optional message items that may be used for cross-border connections are also to be standardized to the extent possible.

(c)    It does not necessarily mean that message items to be used only for specific bilateral linkages or domestic purposes are prohibited.

(d)    ISO 20022 message items that are already in use and/or to be used during implementation need to be honored.

(ii)    ISO 3166 for country codes

ISO 3166 is the international standard for country codes and their subdivisions. The purpose of ISO 3166 is to define internationally recognized codes of letters and/or numbers to refer to countries and subdivisions. ISO 3166 is regularly updated to reflect changes in country names and subdivisions. These changes are done by the ISO 3166 Maintenance Agency. However, it does not define the names of countries; this information comes from United Nations sources. The country codes (ISO 3166-1 Alpha-2) for ASEAN+3 economies are shown in Table 1.

(iii)    ISO 4217 for currency codes

The currency code must be a valid, active currency code. Valid, active currency codes are registered with the ISO 4217 Maintenance Agency and consist of three contiguous letters.[2] The currency codes (ISO 4217) for ASEAN+3 economies are also shown in Table 1.

(iv)    ISO 6166 (ISIN) for securities numbering

ISIN is a numbering system designed by ISO. Each country has a national numbering agency that assigns ISIN numbers for securities in that country. The national numbering agencies for ASEAN+3 economies are shown in Table 1. The Association of National Numbering Agencies is a global association with a common mission.[3]

---

[2]    The maintenance agency is SIX Interbank Clearing on behalf of the Swiss Association for Standardization.

[3]    For details, please refer to the Association of National Numbering Agencies. http://www.anna-web.org/.

**Table 1: ISO Country and Currency Codes, and National Numbering Agencies**

| Economy | ISO Country Code | Currency Code | National Numbering Agency |
|---|---|---|---|
| Brunei Darussalam | BN | BND | Autoriti Monetari Brunei Darussalam (AMBD) |
| Cambodia | KH | KHR | n.a. |
| People's Republic of China | CN | CNY | China Securities Industry Standardization Technology Committee (CSISC) |
| Hong Kong, China | HK | HKD | Hong Kong Exchanges and Clearing Ltd. (HKEx) |
| Indonesia | ID | IDR | Indonesia Central Securities Depository (KSEI) |
| Japan | JP | JPY | Tokyo Stock Exchange (JPX) |
| Republic of Korea | KR | KRW | Korea Exchange (KRX) |
| Lao People's Democratic Republic | LA | LAK | n.a. |
| Malaysia | MY | MYR | Bursa Malaysia Berhad |
| Myanmar | MM | MMK | n.a. |
| Philippines | PH | PHP | Securities and Exchange Commission (SEC) |
| Singapore | SG | SGD | Singapore Exchange Limited (SGX) |
| Thailand | TH | THB | Thailand Securities Depository Co., Ltd. (TSD) |
| Viet Nam | VN | VND | Vietnam Securities Depository (VSD) |

ISO = International Organization for Standardization.
Source: Cross-Border Settlement Infrastructure Forum compilation.

An ISIN comprises a two-character prefix representing the country of issue, followed by a national security number and a check digit. For example, a bond issued in the People's Republic of China (PRC) starts with CN, followed by an eight-digit security number, 08888888, with the check digit, 9, at the end: CN088888889.

(v)    ISO 9362 (BIC) for financial institution identification

A BIC for Financial Institution is registered by the ISO 9362 Registration Authority in the BIC directory.[4] The BIC is an eight-character code, defined as a "business party identifier," consisting of the business party prefix (four alphanumeric characters), the country code as defined in ISO 3166-1 (two alphabetic), and the business party suffix (two alphanumeric characters). The branch identifier is a three-character optional element that can supplement the three-character BIC, used to identify specific locations, departments, services or units of the same business party. Table 2 lists the BIC for financial institutions of CSD and RTGS operators in member economies of ASEAN+3.

---

[4]    The registration authority is Society for Worldwide Interbank Financial Telecommunication (SWIFT).

**Table 2: Business Identifier Codes for Financial Institutions of Central Securities Depository and Real-Time Gross Settlement Operators in ASEAN+3**

| | BICFI (8) | Institution | | BICFI (8) | Institution |
|---|---|---|---|---|---|
| BN | AMBDBNBB | Autoriti Monetari Brunei Darussalam (AMBD) | LA | LPDRLALA | Bank of the Lao PDR (BOL) |
| CN | PBOCCNBJ | People's Bank of China (PBOC) | MM | CBMYMMMY | Central Bank of Myanmar (CBM) |
| | NDCCCNB1 | China Central Depository & Clearing Co., Ltd. (CCDC) | MY | BNMAMY2K | Bank Negara Malaysia (BNM) |
| | CSDACNB1 | China Securities Depository and Clearing Corporation (CSDC) | PH | PHCBPHMA | Bangko Sentral ng Pilipinas (BSP) |
| | CHFMCNSH | Shanghai Clearing House (SHCH) | | BUTRPHM1 | Bureau of the Treasury (BTr) |
| HK | HKMAHKHC | Hong Kong Monetary Authority (HKMA) | | PHCDPHM1 | Philippine Depository and Trust Corp. (PDTC) |
| ID | INDOIDJA | Bank Indonesia (BI) | | ASDBPHMM | Asian Development Bank (ADB) |
| | KSEIIDJA | Indonesia Central Securities Depository (KSEI) | SG | MASGSGSG MASGSGSM | Monetary Authority of Singapore (MAS) |
| JP | BOJPJPJT | Bank of Japan (BOJ) | | CDPLSGSG | The Central Depository (Pte.) Limited (CDP) |
| | JJSDJPJT | Japan Securities Depository Center, Inc. (JASDEC) | TH | BOTHTHB1 | Bank of Thailand (BOT) |
| KH | NCAMKHPP | National Bank of Cambodia (NBC) | | TSDCTHBK | Thai Securities Depository (TSD) |
| KR | BOKRKRSE BOKRKRST | Bank of Korea (BOK) | VN | NABVVNV1 STBVVNVX | State Bank of Vietnam (SBV) |
| | KSDCKRSE | Korea Securities Depository (KSD) | | VISDVNV1 | Vietnam Securities Depository (VSD) |

ASEAN+3 = Association of Southeast Asian Nations plus the People's Republic of China, Japan, and the Republic of Korea; BICFI = Business Identifier Code for Financial Institution; BN = Brunei Darussalam; CN = People's Republic of China; CSD = central securities depository; HK = Hong Kong, China; ID = Indonesia; JP = Japan; KH = Cambodia; KR = Republic of Korea; LA = Lao People's Democratic Republic (Lao PDR); MM = Myanmar; MY = Malaysia; PH = Philippines; RTGS = real-time gross settlement; SG = Singapore; TH =Thailand; VN = Viet Nam.
Source: Asian Development Bank compilation.

(vi)    ISO 8601 for date and time

ISO Date is defined as a particular point in the progression of time in a calendar year expressed in the YYYY-MM-DD format. This representation is defined in the XML Schema Part 2: Datatypes Second Edition—W3C Recommendation, released on 28 October 2004, which is aligned with ISO 8601. ISO Date and Time is defined by a mandatory date and a mandatory time component, expressed in a coordinated universal time format (YYYY-MM-DDThh:mm:ss.sssZ), or in a local time with a coordinated universal time offset format (YYYY-MM-DDThh:mm:ss.sss+/-hh:mm) or a local time format (YYYY-MM-DDThh:mm:ss.sss).

## 2.    User requirements and technical specifications for CSD–RTGS linkage gateways

A)    Outline of user requirements

Possible general user requirements and technical specifications are as follows:

(i) A sufficient level of security, reliability, and availability to connect FMIs in the region bilaterally is necessary:

  (a) To ensure network security and redundancy equivalent across FMIs, FMIs are to be connected with each other through the gateways by secure network such as leased line and secured by sufficient measures such as internet protocol virtual private network.

    i. Security: To prevent information leakage, tampering, and/or repudiation, messages including information sent through the network should be encrypted and marked with a digital signature.

    ii. Reliability: To ensure the reliability of connections between CSD and RTGS systems, message sequencing, retransmission, and idempotency should be adopted.

  (b) Duplication of platform of gateway to back up each other (redundancy).

    i. Availability: To enhance the availability of gateways, active–active or active–standby configurations for gateways should be adopted.

(ii) Implementing measures to avoid negative impacts, such as failures from counterparty, are as follows:

  (a) Individual message instructions are to be processed item by item (message-oriented).

  (b) Appropriate measures to prevent negative impacts from counterparties need to be implemented. Criteria for choosing network providers need to be specified.

(iii) Securing interoperability when connecting FMIs in ASEAN+3 bilaterally includes

  (a) adopting international standards for technical specifications to connect CSD and RTGS systems within the region, and

  (b) implementing the specifications with expandability and flexibility to enable gradual participation in the linkages by the FMIs ready to be connected with each other.

(iv) Functions converting ISO 20022 (ASEAN+3) with ISO 20022 (local standard of each economy) are as follows:

  (a) Mandatory message items of ISO 20022 are to be accepted as mandatory message items with the same definition in all ASEAN+3 economies.

  (b) Optional message items of ISO 20022 for a local economy may be different from those of another economy and/or the ASEAN+3 standard, but they need to be standardized as reasonably as possible.

  (c) Not only message items but also message flows may differ by economy and need to be harmonized as reasonably as possible to absorb differences between the gateways.

(v) Message identification (reference) that can uniquely identify each message for CSD–RTGS linkage end-to-end, even for messages transferred across the economy. An application-based, bilateral, unique, and sequential reference number (temporally named CSD–RTGS interlinking reference) may be introduced.

B)    Possible technical specifications

Technologies and products that are available or will be available in all ASEAN+3 economies in or around 2020 will be adopted.

In order to share a common image of the gateway, possible functions include the following:

    (i)    Communication protocol:

        (a)    With respect to the standard communication protocol for CSD–RTGS linkages, Transmission Control Protocol/Internet Protocol (TCP/IP) is to be adopted since TCP/IP is already the standard communication protocol in ASEAN+3 as well as being adopted by all FMIs in the region.

        (b)    With respect to the communication interface, a loosely connecting interface such as SOAP is to be adopted.[5]

    (ii)    Message format: XML, which is already widely accepted, is to be used. With respect to message types, ISO 20022 compatible messages are to be used in principle.

    (iii)    Character code set: Unicode (UTF-8) is to be used as the character code set.

C)    Interoperability by adopting international standards

The international standards mentioned above should be adopted.

D)    Cross-border network connecting CSD and RTGS systems

Gateways for CSD–RTGS linkages are to be connected to each other bilaterally by commonly used technological measures such as an internet protocol virtual private network. Network providers that are widely used by CSDs and central banks may be adopted as part of the network infrastructure (Figure 5). Basic requirements for network providers of CSD-RTGS linkages are shown in Appendix 2.

E)    Cross-border BCP and cybersecurity

Given the importance of sound and resilient linkages among regional CSD and RTGS operators, it is important that CSIF members maintain the smooth operation of critical business functions and the resiliency of CSD and RTGS systems against potential cyber risks. Gateways for CSD–RTGS linkages need to satisfy the recommendations specified by the CSIF.[6]

---

[5]    Simple object access protocol, or SOAP, has a high level of conformity with XML.

[6]    Asian Development Bank. 2018. *Common Understanding on Cross-Border Business Continuity Planning and Cybersecurity*. Manila.

## Figure 5: Image of Cross-Border Connection

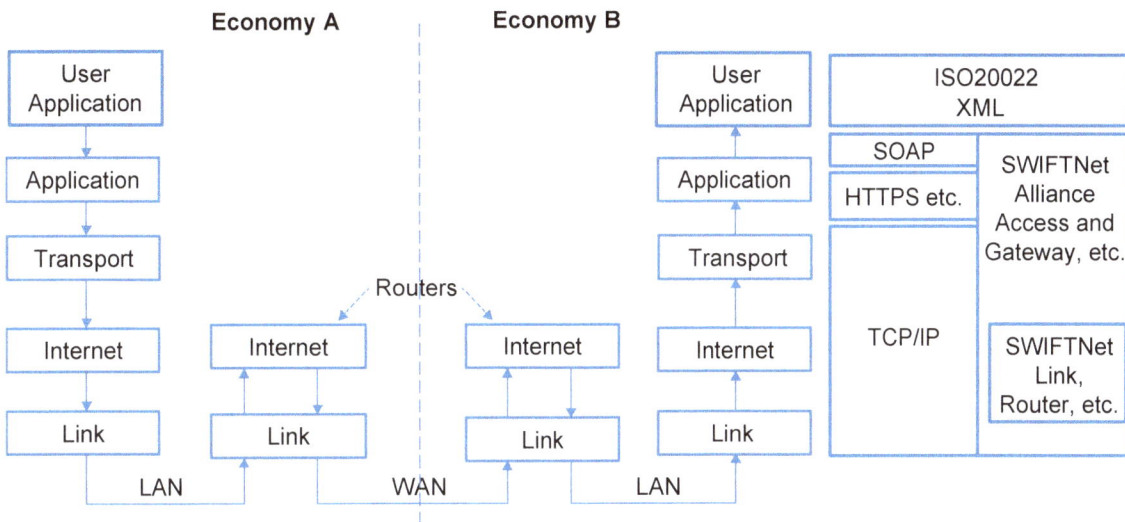

**Economy A**          **Economy B**

| | | | | | |
|---|---|---|---|---|---|
| User Application | | | User Application | | ISO20022 XML |
| Application | | | Application | SOAP / HTTPS etc. | SWIFTNet Alliance Access and Gateway, etc. |
| Transport | | | Transport | | |
| Internet | Internet — Routers | Internet | Internet | TCP/IP | SWIFTNet Link, Router, etc. |
| Link | Link | Link | Link | | |
| LAN | WAN | LAN | | | |

CSD = central securities depository, LAN = local area network, RTGS = real-time gross settlement, SOAP = simple object access protocol, SWIFT = Society for Worldwide Interbank Financial Telecommunication, TCP/IP = transmission control protocol/internet protocol, WAN = wide area network, XML = extensible markup language.

Note: "Internet" refers to the Internet of TCP/IP protocol. As such, the Internet does not have to be the network used for CSD–RTGS linkages.

Source: Asian Development Bank. 2019. *Common Understanding on International Standards and Gateways for Central Securities Depository and Real-Time Gross Settlement*. Manila.

## F)    Other specifications

The following issues need to be considered:

(i)     Version change policy of international standards: ISO 20022 messages are to be reviewed and versions updated annually. A version updating policy needs to be agreed between the parties that are connected by the relevant CSD–RTGS linkages.

(ii)    System performance: Criteria for securing system performance will be discussed and specified.

(iii)   Change management for user requirements and technical specifications: User requirements and technical specifications in this common understanding may be reviewed and updated by taking actual implementation of CSD–RTGS linkages in the region into consideration.

# III. PROGRESS OF CENTRAL SECURITIES DEPOSITORY–REAL-TIME GROSS SETTLEMENT LINKAGE MODELS TO DATE

## A. Potential Benefits of Central Securities Depository–Real-Time Gross Settlement Linkages

CSD–RTGS linkages will connect CSD systems operated by national CSDs and RTGS systems operated by central banks. The linkages allow local currency (LCY) bonds to be settled DVP via central bank money, which ensures the safety of settlement, even in cross-border transactions. Cross-border DVP via CSD–RTGS linkages is compliant with international standards including the Principles for Financial Market Infrastructures of the Committee on Payments and Market Infrastructures. In addition, the linkages will support further cross-border banking and financial integration in ASEAN+3. The ASEAN Economic Community Blueprint 2025 notes that inclusive and stable financial sector development is a key goal of regional economic integration.[7] As a strategic measure, greater market access and operational flexibility for Qualified ASEAN Banks through the ASEAN Banking Integration Framework should be considered. The expected benefits of CSD–RTGS linkages are discussed below.

### 1. Enhancing the financial stability of ASEAN+3

CSD–RTGS linkages can not only reduce cross-border transaction costs but also support risk mitigation by enabling cross-currency DVP and mobilizing LCY government bonds as cross-border collateral. Due to tighter regulations enacted after the global financial crisis, demand for high-quality liquid assets (HQLA) has increased. For cross-border transactions, normally only United States (US) dollars and US Treasury bonds are accepted as HQLA collateral. However, when Asian markets face stress, availability of these may be limited because the US market is not open. Thus, intraregional financial transactions may need to be supported by HQLA within ASEAN+3 markets. CSD–RTGS linkages will support not only trading of LCY government bonds in the region but also utilization of the region's HQLA, hence, alleviating concerns of collateral shortage.

---

[7]  ASEAN Secretariat. 2015. *ASEAN Economic Community Blueprint 2025*. Jakarta.

**2.  Meeting increasing demands for local currency settlement**

Cross-border cash payments and remittances are supported by a correspondent banking network based on US dollars, which inevitably delays payments due to the time difference between markets in Asia and the US market. A remittance between markets in two ASEAN+3 economies will be transferred to the correspondent US banks, settled through the US dollar payment network, and transferred back to Asia—a process that normally takes 2 days (T+2). Along with increasing intraregional trade volume, LCY transactions can potentially be settled more quickly or even the same day. Multicurrency cash management may be necessary because barriers between LCY markets in ASEAN+3 economies will persist for some time. In such circumstances, CSD–RTGS linkages, which directly connect central bank RTGS systems, would help support efficient and spontaneous cash delivery between ASEAN+3 markets.

There are some leading cases of CSD–RTGS linkages in the region. The following sections will explain the notable features of (i) cross-border DVP between the Bank of Japan and the Hong Kong Monetary Authority's (HKMA); (ii) Bond Connect as a CSD–CSD linkage between China Central Depository & Clearing Co., Ltd. (CCDC) and Shanghai Clearing House (SHCH) in the PRC and the HKMA; and (ii) PVP linkages between the HKMA and markets in some ASEAN economies. The CSIF discussions have focused on how these leading cases can provide a basis to expand standardized messages and practices in the region. Thus, the reference flows shown in Figures 7, 9, and 11 will be reviewed and revised along with the changes in the technological environment and transactions in the region.

## B.    Cross-Border Delivery Versus Payment Linkages

The Bank of Japan and the HKMA are developing cross-border DVP links by connecting the Bank of Japan Financial Network System Japanese Government Bond services with the Hong Kong Dollar Clearing House Automated Transfer System, known as Hong Kong dollar CHATS, which is the RTGS for Hong Kong dollars. The link, which will enable DVP settlement of Japanese Government Bonds and Hong Kong dollars, will go live in spring 2021. Cross-border DVP will eliminate settlement risk arising from differences in time zones and jurisdictions and will facilitate cross-currency repurchase agreements (repo). Figure 6 illustrates how financial institution A can transfer Japanese Government Bonds to financial institution B in return for simultaneous Hong Kong dollar funding from financial institution B to A.

Figure 7 shows the outline of CSD–RTGS Linkages for Cross-Currency Delivery Versus Payment published in the progress report in 2015.

The harmonization of message flows would be necessary to expand cross-border DVP linkages in the region. Among the message items, transaction identifications are needed to ensure smooth cross-border settlement between CSD and RTGS. In addition, the sending date and operating hours need to be harmonized.

## Figure 6: Cross-Border Delivery Versus Payment

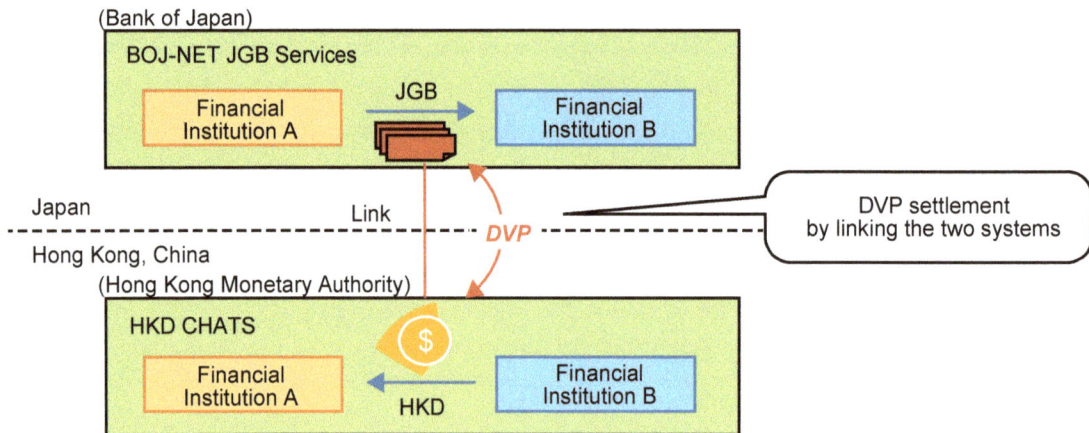

BOJ = Bank of Japan, BOJ-NET = Bank of Japan Financial Network System, CHATS = Clearing House Automated Transfer System, DVP = delivery versus payment, HKD = Hong Kong dollar, JGB = Japanese Government Bond.

Source: Bank of Japan. 2018. *Preparation for the Implementation of Cross-Border DVP Link between BOJ-NET JGB Services and HKD CHATS*. Tokyo.

## Figure 7: Outline of Central Securities Depository–Real-Time Gross Settlement Linkages for Cross-Currency Delivery Versus Payment

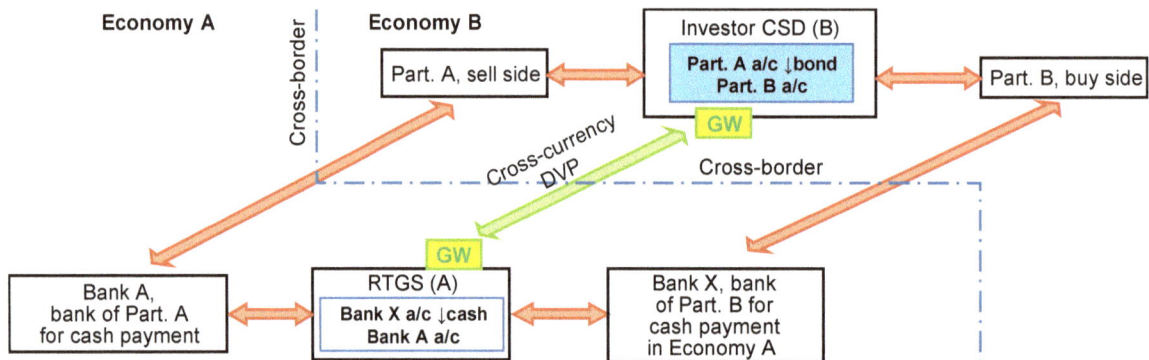

a/c = account, CSD = central securities depository, DVP = delivery versus payment, RTGS = real-time gross settlement.

Notes:
1. The investor, participant B of CSD (B) in economy B, sends a buy local currency B bond instruction to CSD (B) and instructs bank X, cash payment bank of the participant B, to pay in local currency A to bank A. Bank A is the cash payment bank of the participant A of CSD (B).
2. Within CSD (B), participant A sends a sell bond instruction to CSD (B) indicating the details of the transaction.
3. Within CSD (B), CSD (B) matches the instructions from participant A and participant B. After matching, CSD (B) earmarks (locks) the bond in the account of participant A, and then sends cash settlement data to RTGS (A).
4. RTGS (A) forwards the transaction (data) from CSD (B) to bank X for affirmation.
5. After receiving the affirmation from bank X, RTGS (A) transfers funds from bank X's account to bank A's account. Then, RTGS (A) sends the cash settlement completion information to CSD (B) as well as bank A and bank X.
6. Within CSD (B), CSD (B) transfers the earmarked (locked) bond to participant B's account.
7. CSD (B) sends bond settlement completion information to participant A and participant B.

Source: Asian Development Bank Consultant for the Cross-Border Settlement Infrastructure Forum (CSIF).

## C.    Central Securities Depository–Central Securities Depository Linkages

Bond Connect is an arrangement that enables investors in the PRC and Hong Kong, China to trade, settle, and hold bonds between the two markets by linking CCDC and SHCH in the PRC with the HKMA's Central Moneymarkets Unit (CMU).[8] In addition to the settlement link, Hong Kong Exchanges and Clearing Limited and the China Foreign Exchange Trade System & National Interbank Funding Center (CFETS) provide a cross-border electronic bond trading platform (Figure 8). The initial phase of Bond Connect commenced on 3 July 2017, enabling investors from Hong Kong, China, to invest in the China Interbank Bond Market.

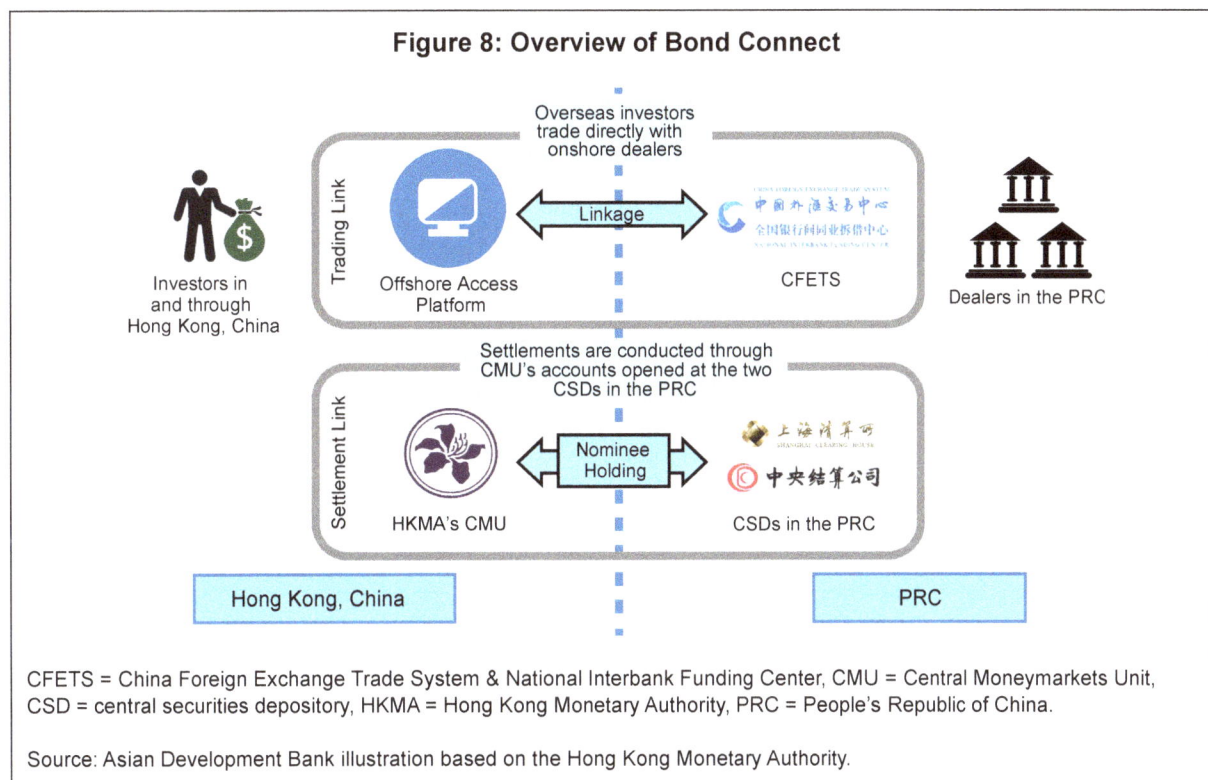

**Figure 8: Overview of Bond Connect**

CFETS = China Foreign Exchange Trade System & National Interbank Funding Center, CMU = Central Moneymarkets Unit, CSD = central securities depository, HKMA = Hong Kong Monetary Authority, PRC = People's Republic of China.

Source: Asian Development Bank illustration based on the Hong Kong Monetary Authority.

Under Bond Connect, the CMU opens an omnibus account with CCDC and SHCH, so the CMU can settle on behalf of its members. Overseas investors who have an account at the CMU can trade directly with onshore dealers via the offshore access platform linking with CFETS. After a trade is completed, the trade details will be sent from CFETS to the two CSDs, which in turn will provide trade details. Then, the investor sends the trade details via a CMU member terminal or the Society for Worldwide Interbank Financial Telecommunication (SWIFT) to a CMU member custodian. When the CMU receives the trade details from the CSD, the CMU will confirm the trade details from the CSD by using the trade information provided by the investors through a CMU member custodian to the CMU system.

---

[8]    Bond Connect Company Limited. https://www.chinabondconnect.com/en/index.htm.

Figure 9 shows the outline of cross-border CSD linkage with domestic delivery versus payment published in the progress report in 2015.

**Figure 9: Outline of Cross-Border Central Securities Depository Linkage with Domestic Delivery Versus Payment**

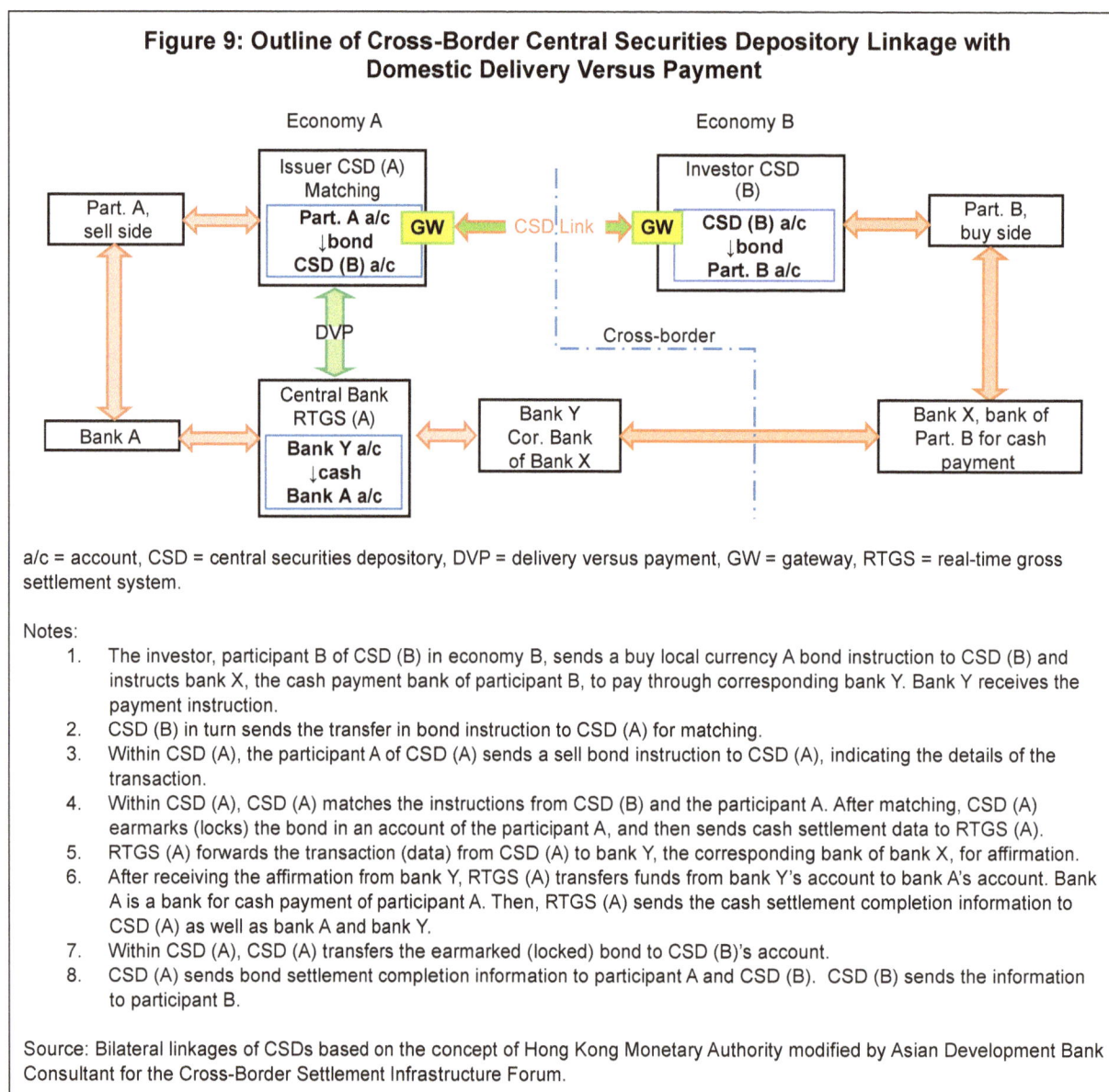

a/c = account, CSD = central securities depository, DVP = delivery versus payment, GW = gateway, RTGS = real-time gross settlement system.

Notes:
1. The investor, participant B of CSD (B) in economy B, sends a buy local currency A bond instruction to CSD (B) and instructs bank X, the cash payment bank of participant B, to pay through corresponding bank Y. Bank Y receives the payment instruction.
2. CSD (B) in turn sends the transfer in bond instruction to CSD (A) for matching.
3. Within CSD (A), the participant A of CSD (A) sends a sell bond instruction to CSD (A), indicating the details of the transaction.
4. Within CSD (A), CSD (A) matches the instructions from CSD (B) and the participant A. After matching, CSD (A) earmarks (locks) the bond in an account of the participant A, and then sends cash settlement data to RTGS (A).
5. RTGS (A) forwards the transaction (data) from CSD (A) to bank Y, the corresponding bank of bank X, for affirmation.
6. After receiving the affirmation from bank Y, RTGS (A) transfers funds from bank Y's account to bank A's account. Bank A is a bank for cash payment of participant A. Then, RTGS (A) sends the cash settlement completion information to CSD (A) as well as bank A and bank Y.
7. Within CSD (A), CSD (A) transfers the earmarked (locked) bond to CSD (B)'s account.
8. CSD (A) sends bond settlement completion information to participant A and CSD (B).  CSD (B) sends the information to participant B.

Source: Bilateral linkages of CSDs based on the concept of Hong Kong Monetary Authority modified by Asian Development Bank Consultant for the Cross-Border Settlement Infrastructure Forum.

## D.    Payment Versus Payment Linkages

Cross-border bilateral PVP linkages directly connect RTGS systems located in different economies. The definition of PVP is "a settlement mechanism that ensures that the final transfer of a payment in one currency occurs if and only if the final transfer of a payment in another currency or currencies takes place."[9]

---

[9]    The Bank for International Settlements (BIS) glossary is available at https://www.bis.org/cpmi/publ/d00b.htm.

The HKMA and Hong Kong Interbank Clearing Limited have been operating PVP for years connecting mainly domestic RTGS systems and some cross-border RTGS systems (Figure 10).

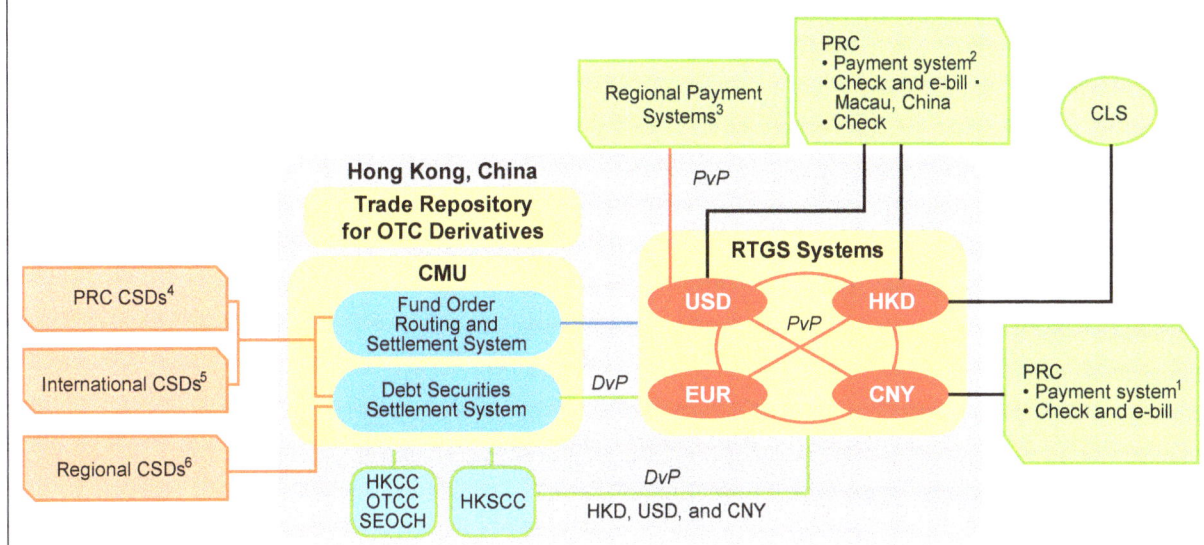

**Figure 10: Payment Versus Payment Linkages in Hong Kong, China**

CCDC = China Central Depository & Clearing Co. Ltd. (settlement system for fixed income securities in China), CDFCPS = China's Domestic Foreign Currency Payment System in China. CIPS = Cross-border Interbank Payment System in China, CLS = Continuous Linked Settlement (global multicurrency cash settlement system), CMU = Central Moneymarkets Unit (settlement system for debt securities), CNAPS = China National Advanced Payment System (CNY RTGS system in China), CSD = central securities depository, DVP = delivery versus payment, CSDC = China Securities Depository & Clearing Corporation., Ltd., EUR = euro, HKCC = HKFE Clearing Corp Ltd (central counterparty providing clearing and settlement for futures), HKD = Hong Kong dollar, HKSCC = Hong Kong Securities Clearing Co Ltd (operator of the clearing and settlement system for shares), KSD = Korea Securities Depository (Republic of Korea's central securities depository), OTC = over-the-counter, OTCC = OTC Clearing in Hong Kong Limited (central counterparty providing clearing and settlement for OTC derivatives), PRC = People's Republic of China, PVP = payment versus payment, CNY = Yuan Renminbi, RTGS = real-time gross settlement, SEOCH = SEHK Options Clearing House Ltd (central counterparty providing clearing and settlement for options), SHCH = Shanghai Clearing House (settlement system for fixed income securities in China), SZFSS = Shenzhen Financial Settlement System, TDCC = Taipei,China's securities settlement system, USD = United States dollar.

[1] CNAPS, CIPS, and SZFSS
[2] CDFCPS, RTGS links with Shenzhen and Guangdong
[3] PVP links with Malaysia, Thailand, and Indonesia
[4] Cross-border links with CCDC and SHCH (Bond Connect) and CSDC (Mutual Recognition of Funds)
[5] Cross-border links with Clearstream and Euroclear
[6] Cross-border links with Austraclear (Australia), KSD (Republic of Korea) and TDCC (Taipei,China)

Source: Hong Kong Monetary Authority.

The HKMA and Hong Kong Interbank Clearing Limited are enhancing the interoperability of their PVP by adopting international standards such as ISO 20022. Figure 11 shows the outline of RTGS–RTGS linkages for payment versus payment published in the progress report in 2015.

**Figure 11: Outline of Real-Time Gross Settlement–Real-Time Gross Settlement Linkages for Payment Versus Payment**

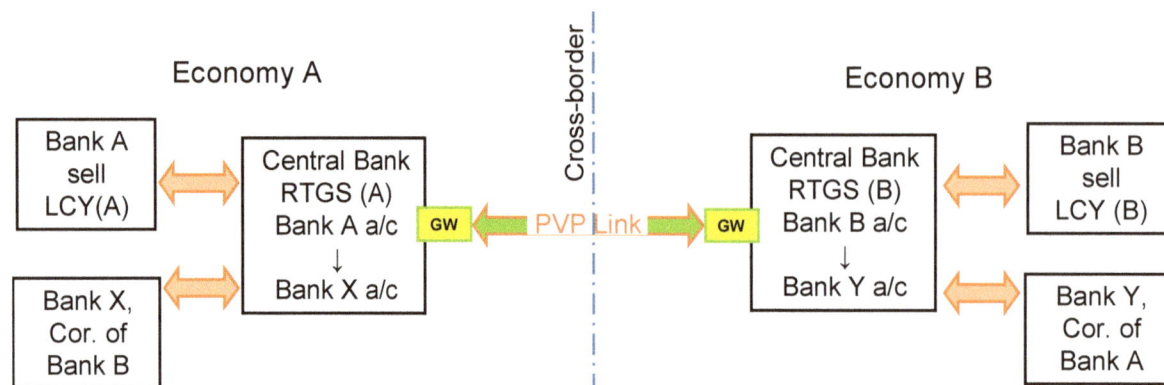

a/c = account, GW = gateway, LCY = local currency, PVP = payment versus payment, RTGS = real-time gross settlement.

Notes:
1. Bank A in economy A sends a sell local currency A and buy local currency B instruction to RTGS (A). Bank B in economy B sends a sell local currency B and buy local currency A instruction to RTGS (B).
2. RTGS (A) and RTGS (B) forward the information to gateways in economy A and economy B, respectively.
3. The gateways exchange and match the information.
4. When matched, each gateway sends an instruction to each RTGS to hold (earmark or block) the local currency funds of each economy.
5. After holding the funds, each RTGS sends a holding completion message to the gateway. The gateways exchange information with each other and confirm the holding of funds.
6. Each gateway forwards the information to the appropriate RTGS.
7. Each RTGS releases the held funds (local currency A to bank X's account and local currency B to bank Y's account).
8. Fund settlement confirmation is sent to bank A and bank B as well as counterparty RTGS through the gateways.

Source: Bilateral linkages of RTGS systems based on the concept of Hong Kong Monetary Authority modified by Asian Development Bank Consultant for the Cross-Border Settlement Infrastructure Forum.

# IV. PROGRESS OF STANDARDIZATION IN ASEAN+3

Major financial markets, including in Europe and the US, have announced the adoption of ISO 20022 for major FMIs. The Eurosystem's Vision 2020 promotes ISO 20022. In 2014, the Federal Reserve and the Clearing House announced their intention to adopt ISO 20022 in payment messages for Fedwire and the Clearing House Interbank Payments System. The PRC, India, Japan, and the Russian Federation have already implemented ISO 20022 in their FMIs. Thanks to the efforts of CSIF members, ASEAN+3 economies are now ready to implement the international standard. CSD and RTGS system operators in the region are supporting their participants' migration to ISO 20022. The related discussions focus more on how to maximize the expandability of data exchanges under ISO 20022.

## A. Outline of Central Securities Depository and Real-Time Gross Settlement Systems in ASEAN+3

CSD systems for government bonds are already operating in all ASEAN+3 economies except Cambodia and the Lao People's Democratic Republic (Lao PDR), where book-entry systems for government bonds are under planning and development. CSD systems for corporate bonds are already operating in all ASEAN+3 economies except the Lao PDR and Myanmar. In the case of Cambodia, a few corporate bonds have already been issued and can be traded in the exchange market. Having said that, an appropriate CSD system for corporate bonds which can settle bonds with DVP model 1 has not been implemented yet. RTGS systems are already operating in all ASEAN+3 economies.[10] Government bonds are settled using central bank money. Both government bonds and corporate bonds are traded mostly in over-the-counter (OTC) markets in ASEAN+3 economies. Significant volumes of government bonds are traded on exchanges in the Republic of Korea and the Philippines, though the majority of trading volume occurs in OTC markets (Figures 12, 13).

---

[10] RTGS system in Cambodia will be live by the time this progress report is published.

## Figure 12: ASEAN+3 Government Bond Market Diagram

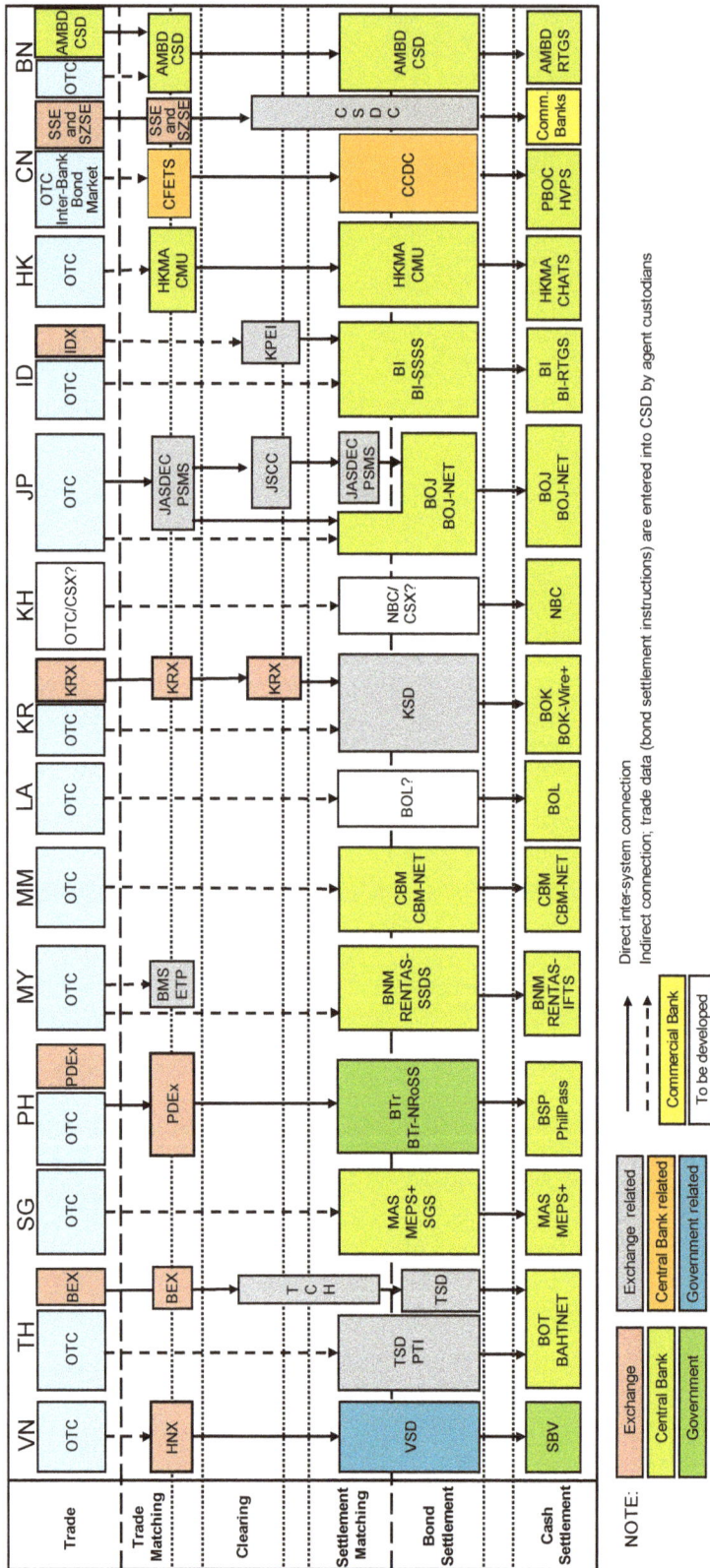

NOTE:

Exchange
Central Bank
Government

Exchange-related
Central Bank related
Government related

Commercial Bank
To be developed

Direct inter-system connection
Indirect connection; trade data (bond settlement instructions) are entered into CSD by agent custodians

AMBD = Autoriti Monetari Brunei Darussalam; ASEAN = Association of Southeast Asian Nations; ASEAN+3 = ASEAN plus the People's Republic of China, Japan, and the Republic of Korea; BAHTNET = Bank of Thailand Automated High-value Transfer Network; BEX = Bond Electronic Exchange; BI = Bank Indonesia; BI-SSSS = Bank Indonesia-Scripless Securities Settlement System; BMS = Bursa Malaysia Securities; BN = Brunei Darussalam; BNM = Bank Negara Malaysia; BOJ = Bank of Japan; BOK = Bank of Korea; BOL = Bank of the Lao PDR; BOT = Bank of Thailand; BSP = Bangko Sentral ng Pilipinas; BTr-NRoSS = Bureau of the Treasury; BTr-NRoSS = Bureau of the Treasury National Registry of Scripless Securities; CBM = Central Bank of Myanmar; CCDC = China Central Depository & Clearing Co., Ltd.; CFETS = China Foreign Exchange and Trade System; CHATS = Clearing House Automated Transfer System; CMU = Central Moneymarkets Unit; CN = People's Republic of China; CSD = Central Securities Depository; CSDC = China Securities Depository and Clearing Corporation Limited; ETP = Electronic Trading Platform; HK = Hong Kong, China; HKMA = Hong Kong Monetary Authority; HNX = Hanoi Stock Exchange; HVPS = High-Value Payment System; ID = Indonesia; IDX = Indonesia Stock Exchange; JASDEC = Japan Securities Depository Center, Inc.; JP = Japan; JSCC = Japan Securities Clearing Corporation; KH = Cambodia; KPEI = PT Kliring Penjaminan Efek Indonesia (Indonesia Clearing and Guarantee Corporation); KR = Republic of Korea; KRX = Korea Exchange; KSD = Korea Securities Depository; LA = Lao People's Democratic Republic; MAS = Monetary Authority of Singapore; MEPS = MAS Electronic Payment System; MM = Myanmar; MY = Malaysia; NBC = National Bank of Cambodia; OTC = over-the-counter; PBOC = People's Bank of China; PDEx = Philippine Dealing & Exchange Corp.; PDTC = Philippine Depository & Trust Corp.; PH = Philippines; PhilPass = Philippine Payment and Settlement System; PSMS = Pre-Settlement Matching System; PTI = Post Trade Integration System; RENTAS-IFTS = Real-Time Electronic Transfer of Funds and Securities - Interbank Funds Transfer System; RENTAS-SSDS = Real-Time Electronic Transfer of Funds and Securities - Scripless Securities Depository System; RoSS = Registry of Scripless Securities; RTGS = real-time gross settlement; SBV = State Bank of Vietnam; SG = Singapore; SGS = Singapore Government Securities; SSE = Shanghai Stock Exchange; STP = straight-through-processing; SZSE = Shenzhen Stock Exchange; TCH = Thailand Clearing House Co. Ltd.; TH = Thailand; TSD = Thailand Securities Depository; VN = Viet Nam; VSD = Vietnam Securities Depository.

Source: Based on Asian Development Bank. 2013. ASEAN+3 Information on Transaction Flows and Settlement Infrastructures. Manila, updated by ADB consultant.

## Figure13: ASEAN+3 Corporate Bond Market Diagram

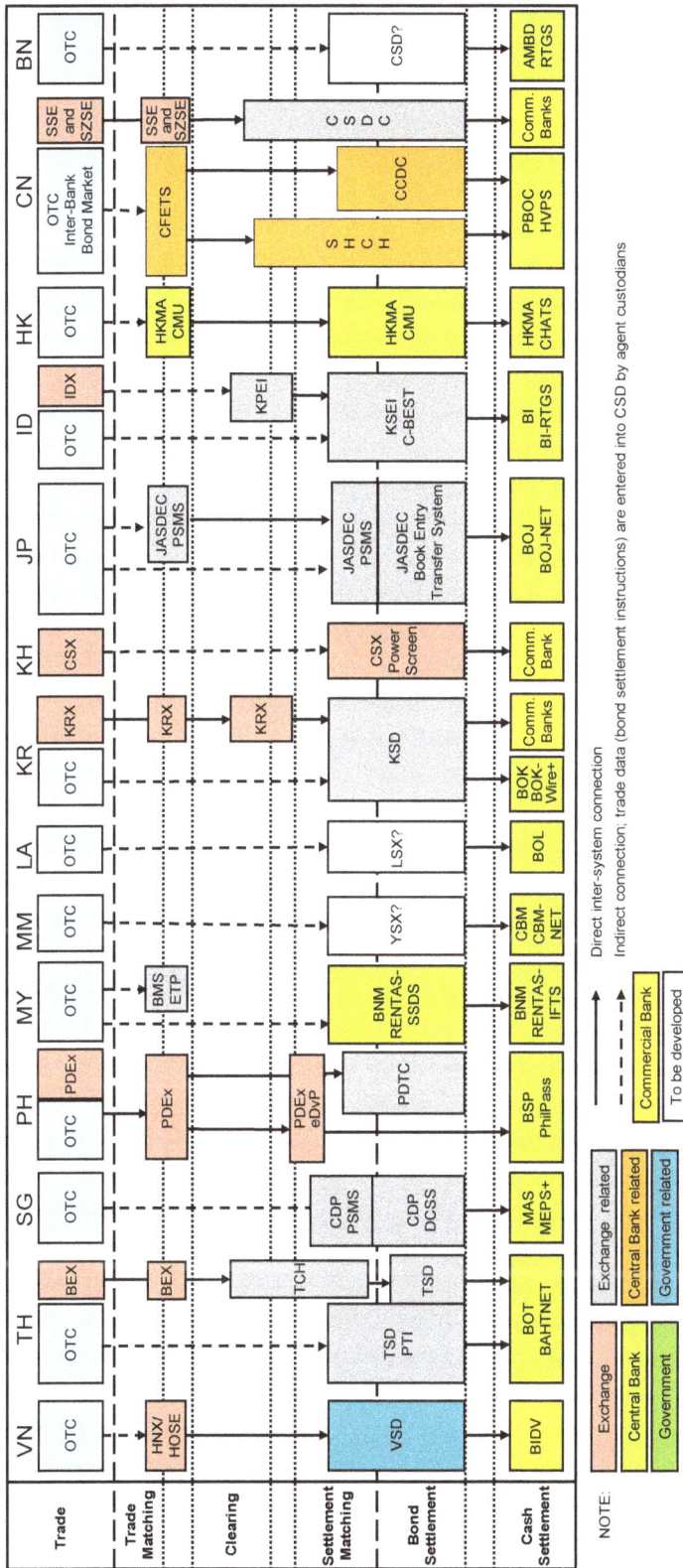

NOTE:

→ Direct inter-system connection

--- Indirect connection; trade data (bond settlement instructions) are entered into CSD by agent custodians

Exchange related
Central Bank related
Government related

Exchange
Central Bank
Government

AMBD = Autoriti Monetari Brunei Darussalam; ASEAN = Association of Southeast Asian Nations; ASEAN+3 = ASEAN plus the People's Republic of China, Japan, and the Republic of Korea; BAHTNET = Bank of Thailand Automated High-value Transfer Network; BEX = Bond Electronic Exchange; BI = Bank Indonesia; BI-RTGS = Bank Indonesia Real Time Gross Settlement; BIDV = Bank of Investment and Development of Viet Nam; BMS = Bursa Malaysia Securities; BN = Brunei Darussalam; BNM = Bank Negara Malaysia; BOJ = Bank of Japan; BOJ-NET = Bank of Japan Financial Network System; BOK = Bank of Korea; BOL = Bank of the Lao PDR; BOT = Bank of Thailand; BSP = Bangko Sentral ng Pilipinas; C-BEST = Central Depository and Book Entry Settlement System; CBM = Central Bank of Myanmar; CCDC = China Central Depository & Clearing Co., Ltd.; CDP = Central Depository; CFETS = China Foreign Exchange and Trade System; CHATS = Clearing House Automated Transfer System; CMU = Central Moneymarkets Unit; CN = People's Republic of China; CSD = central securities depository; CSDC = China Securities Depository and Clearing Corporation Limited; CSX = Cambodia Securities Exchange; DCSS = Debt Securities Clearing Settlement Systems; eDVP = expanded Delivery versus Payment; ETP = Electronic Trading Platform; HK = Hong Kong, China; HKMA = Hong Kong Monetary Authority; HNX = Hanoi Stock Exchange; HOSE = Ho Chi Minh Stock Exchange; HVPS = High-Value Payment System; ID = Indonesia, IDX = Indonesia Stock Exchange; JASDEC = Japan Securities Depository Center, Inc.; JP = Japan; KH = Cambodia; KR = Republic of Korea; KPEI = PT Kliring Penjaminan Efek Indonesia (Indonesia Clearing and Guarantee Corporation); KRX = Korea Exchange; KSD = Korea Securities Depository; KSEI = Kustodian Sentral Efek Indonesia (Indonesia Central Securities Depository); LA = Lao People's Democratic Republic; LSX = Lao Stock Exchange; MAS = Monetary Authority of Singapore; MEPS = MAS Electronic Payment System; MM = Myanmar; MY = Malaysia; OTC = over-the-counter; PBOC = People's Bank of China; PDEx = Philippine Dealing & Exchange Corp.; PDTC = Philippine Depository & Trust Corp.; PH = Philippines; PhilPass = Philippine Payment and Settlement System; PSMS = Pre-Settlement Matching System; PTI = Post Trade Integration; RENTAS-IFTS = Real-Time Electronic Transfer of Funds and Securities - Interbank Funds Transfer System; RENTAS-SSDS = Real-Time Electronic Transfer of Funds and Securities - Scripless Securities Depository System; RTGS = real-time gross settlement; SG = Singapore; SHCH = Shanghai Clearing House; SSE = Shanghai Stock Exchange; SZSE = Shenzhen Stock Exchange; TCH = Thailand Clearing House Co. Ltd.; TH = Thailand; TSD = Thailand Securities Depository; VN = Viet Nam; VSD = Vietnam Securities Depository; YSX = Yangon Stock Exchange.

Source: Based on Asian Development Bank. 2013. *ASEAN+3 Information on Transaction Flows and Settlement Infrastructures*. Manila, updated by ADB consultant

## B.    Adoption of ISO 20022

The owners and operators of CSD and RTGS systems in ASEAN+3 are adopting international standards such as ISO 20022 as the message standard to secure interoperability with other systems, particularly for cross-border connections. Adoption of ISO 20022 for the CSD and RTGS systems under operation is shown in Table 3.

**Table 3: Central Securities Depository Systems in ASEAN+3 Economies**

| | CSD (Type of Organization) | Name of System | Gov. or Corp. Bond | Year of Operation | Online Local Time Operating Hours (Time Difference from Jakarta) | ISO 20022 Local Approach (Plan) | ISO 20022 Cross-Border |
|---|---|---|---|---|---|---|---|
| BN | AMBD (CB&GA) | CSD | Gov. | 2017 | 9:00 a.m.– 4:45 p.m. (+1)[1] | Y: big bang | Y |
| CN | CCDC (CbR) | CBGS | Both | 2013 | 9:00 a.m.–5:00 p.m. (+1) | Y: big bang | Y |
| CN | CSDC (ExR) | MNS | Corp. | 2011 | 8:00 a.m.–4:00 p.m. (+1) | Y (202X) | Y (202X) |
| CN | SHCH (ExR) | SHCH-SSS | Corp. | 2011 | 9:00 a.m.–5:00 p.m. (+1) | Y (202X) | Y (202X) |
| HK | HKMA (CB& GA) | CMU | Both | 1990 | 8:30 a.m.–6:20 p.m. (+1) | Y (2022) | Y (2022) |
| ID | BI (CB) | BI-SSSS | Gov. | 2003 | 7:30 a.m.–8:00 p.m. (0) | Y (202X) | Y (202X) |
| ID | KSEI (ExR) | C-BEST | Corp. | | 4:00 a.m.–5:10 p.m. (0) | Y (202X) | Y (202X) |
| JP | BOJ (CB) | BOJ-NET JGB Services | Gov. | 2015 | 8:30 a.m.–9:00 p.m. (+2) | Y: big bang | Y |
| JP | JASDEC (ExR) | BETS | Corp. | 2014 | 9:00 a.m.–5:00 p.m. (+2) | Y: 5 year coex. | Y |
| KH | CSX (Ex) | (Power Screen) | Corp. | 2018 | 8:00 a.m.-3:00 p.m. (0) | n.a. | n.a. |
| KR | KSD (ExR) | SSS/e-SAFE | Both | 2011 | 9:00 a.m.–5:30 p.m. (+2) | n.a. | Y (2020) |
| MM | CBM (CB) | CBM-NET CSD | Gov. | 2016 | 9:30 a.m.–3:00 p.m. (−0.5) | Y (2020) | Y (2020) |
| MY | BNM (CB) | RENTAS-SSDS | Both | 1999 | 8:00 a.m.–6:00 p.m. (+1) | Y (202X) | Y (202X) |
| PH | BTr (GA) | BTr-NRoSS | Gov. | 1996[2] | 9:00 a.m.–6:00 p.m. (+1) | Y (202X) | Y (202X) |
| PH | PDTC (ExR) | PDTC | Corp. | 1995 | 8:00 a.m.–6:00 p.m. (+1) | Y (2021) | Y (2021) |
| SG | MAS (CB&GA) | MEPS+ SGS | Gov. | 2006 | 9:00 a.m.–7:00 p.m. (+1) | Y (202X) | Y |
| SG | CDP (ExR) | DCSS | Corp. | 2015 | 8:30 a.m.–5:30 p.m. (+1) | Y | Y |
| TH | TSD (ExR) | PTI | Both | 2007 | 7:00 a.m.–8:30 p.m. (0) | Y (2021) | Y (2021) |
| VN | VSD[3] | VSD-BES | Both | 2010 | 8:00 a.m.–5:00 p.m. (0) | Y (2025) | Y(202X) |

AMBD = Autoriti Monetari Brunei Darussalam; BES = book-entry system; BETS = Book Entry Transfer Systems; BI = Bank Indonesia; BI-SSSS = Bank Indonesia-Scripless Securities Settlement System; BN = Brunei Darussalam; BNM = Bank Negara Malaysia; BOJ = Bank of Japan; BOJ-NET = Bank of Japan Financial Network System; BTr = Bureau of the Treasury; BTr-NRoSS = Bureau of the Treasury National Registry of Scripless Securities; C-BEST = Central Depository and Book Entry Settlement System; CB = central bank; CBGS = Central Bond General System; CBM = Central Bank of Myanmar; CBM-NET = Central Bank of Myanmar Financial Network System; CbR = central-bank-related organization; CCDC = China Central Depository & Clearing Co., Ltd.; CDP = Central Depository; CMU = Central Moneymarkets Unit; CN = People's Republic of China; CSD = central securities depository; CSDC = China Securities Depository and Clearing Corporation Limited; CSX = Cambodia Securities Exchange; DCSS = Debt Securities Clearing and Settlement System; e-SAFE = Speedy, Accurate, Faithful, Efficient (KSD's system); ExR = exchange-related organization; GA = government agency; HK = Hong Kong, China; HKMA = Hong Kong Monetary Authority; ID = Indonesia; JASDEC = Japan Securities Depository Center, Inc.; JGB = Japanese Government Bond; JP = Japan; KR = Republic of Korea; KSD = Korea Securities Depository; KSEI = Kustodian Sentral Efek Indonesia (Indonesia Central Securities Depository); MAS = Monetary Authority of Singapore; MEPS+ = MAS Electronic Payment System; MM = Myanmar; MNS = Multilateral Net Settlement System; MY = Malaysia; n.a. = not applicable; PDTC = Philippine Depository & Trust Corp.; PH = Philippines; PTI = Post Trade Integration; SG = Singapore; RENTAS-SSDS = Real-Time Electronic Transfer of Funds and Securities - Scripless Securities Depository System; SGS = Singapore Government Securities; SHCH = Shanghai Clearing House; SSS = Securities Settlement System; TH =Thailand; TSD = Thailand Securities Depository; VN = Viet Nam; VSD = Vietnam Securities Depository.

[1.] AMBD's CSD has shorter operating hours during Friday and Ramadhan.
[2.] BTr-ROSS (started operating in 1996) was replaced with a new system BTr-NRoSS in August 2018.
[3.] VSD (wholly state-owned limited liability company).

Source: Based on Asian Development Bank. 2013. ASEAN+3 *Information on Transaction Flows and Settlement Infrastructures*. Manila.

**Table 4: Real-Time Gross Settlement (High-Value) Systems in ASEAN+3 Economies**

| | Operator | Name of System | Current System Started | Online Local Time Operating Hours (Time Difference from Jakarta) | ISO 20022 Local Approach (Plan) | ISO 20022 Cross-Border |
|---|---|---|---|---|---|---|
| BN | AMBD | RTGS | 2014 | 9:00 a.m.–5:00 p.m. (+1)[1] | Y: big bang | Y |
| CN | PBOC | CIPS2 | 2018 | 0:00 a.m.–11:59 p.m. (+1) | Y: big bang | Y |
| HK | HKMA | CHATS | 1996 | 8:00 a.m.–6:00 p.m. (+1) | Y (2022) | Y (2022) |
| ID | BI | BI-RTGS | 2000 | 7:00 a.m.–5:30 p.m. (0) | Y (202X) | Y (202X) |
| JP | BOJ | BOJ-NET FTS | 2015 | 8:30 a.m.–9:00 p.m. (+2) | Y: big bang | Y |
| KH | NBC | - | 2020 | (to be confirmed) | Y | Y |
| KR | BOK | BOK-Wire+ | 2009 | 9:00 a.m.–5:30 p.m. (+2) | n. a. | Y (2021) |
| LA | BOL | - | 2019 | 9:00 a.m.–3:30 p.m. (0) | Y | Y |
| MM | CBM | CBM-NET FTS | 2016 | 9:30 a.m.–3:00 p.m. (–0.5) | Y (2020) | Y (2020) |
| MY | BNM | RENTAS-IFTS | 2011 | 8:00 a.m.–6:00 p.m. (+1) | Y (202X) | Y (202X) |
| PH | BSP | PhilPaSS | 2002 | 9:00 a.m.–5:45 p.m. (+1) | Y (2021) | Y (2021) |
| SG | MAS | MEPS+ | 2006 | 9:00 a.m.–5:30 p.m. (+1) | Y (202X) | Y (202X) |
| TH | BOT | BAHTNET | 2013 | 9:00 a.m.–5:00 p.m. (0) | Y (2022) | Y (2022) |
| VN | SBV | IBPS | 2010 | 8:00 a.m. –5:00 p.m. (0) [2] | Y (2025) | Y (202X) |

AMBD = Autoriti Monetari Brunei Darussalam; BAHTNET = Bank of Thailand Automated High-value Transfer Network; BI = Bank Indonesia; BI-RTGS = Bank Indonesia Real Time Gross Settlement; BN = Brunei Darussalam; BNM = Bank Negara Malaysia; BOJ = Bank of Japan; BOJ-NET = Bank of Japan Financial Network System; BOJ-NET FTS = BOJ-NET Funds Transfer System; BOK = Bank of Korea; BOK-Wire+ = Bank of Korea Financial Wire Network; BOL = Bank of the Lao PDR; BOT = Bank of Thailand; BSP = Bangko Sentral ng Pilipinas; CBM = Central Bank of Myanmar; CBM-NET = Central Bank of Myanmar Financial Network System; CBM-NET FTS = CBM-NET Funds Transfer Service; CbR = central-bank-related organization; CHATS = clearing house automated transfer system; CIPS = cross-border interbank payment system; CN = People's Republic of China; ExR = exchange-related organization; GA = government agency; HK = Hong Kong, China; HKMA = Hong Kong Monetary Authority; IBPS = interbank electronic payment system; ID = Indonesia; JP = Japan; KH = Cambodia; KR = Republic of Korea; LA = Lao People's Democratic Republic (Lao PDR); MAS = Monetary Authority of Singapore; MEPS+ = MAS Electronic Payment System; MM = Myanmar; MY = Malaysia; n.a. = not applicable; NBC = National Bank of Cambodia; PBOC = People's Bank of China; PH = Philippines; PhilPass = Philippine Payment and Settlement System; RTGS = real-time gross settlement system; RENTAS-IFTS = real-time electronic transfer of funds and securities - interbank funds transfer system; SBV = State Bank of Vietnam; SG = Singapore; TH =Thailand; VN = Viet Nam.

[1] AMBD's RTGS has shorter operating hours during Friday and Ramadhan.
[2] SBV IBPS's operating hours are from 8:00 a.m. to 5:00 p.m. on a normal working day and until 5:45 p.m. on the last two working days of the month.

Source: Based on Asian Development Bank. 2013. *ASEAN+3 Information on Transaction Flows and Settlement Infrastructures.* Manila.

## C.    Remaining Challenges for More Standardized Markets

The CSIF conducted a survey on the features and functions of cross-border connections such as adoption of XML, DVP model including real-time function, blocking securities, matching, operating hours, and BCP. To fully implement CSD–RTGS linkages in the region, it is necessary to make further efforts with regard to the following features.

### 1.    ISO 20022 (XML)

XML is a technology (language) used to specify ISO 20022. With respect to government bond CSD systems, three economies (Brunei Darussalam, the PRC, and Japan) have already implemented XML. All other economies in ASEAN+3 will be able to implement this technology by or around 2023.

Regarding corporate bond CSD systems, three economies (the PRC, Japan, and Singapore) have already implemented this feature. All other economies in ASEAN+3 will hopefully have implemented XML for a corporate bond CSD system by or around 2023.

Those economies in the region with the least developed bond markets—including Cambodia, the Lao PDR, and Myanmar—are expected to catch up with the others by implementing the necessary FMI.

## 2.    DVP model 1 with RTGS function

For government bond markets, 12 economies (Brunei Darussalam; the PRC; Hong Kong, China; Indonesia; Japan; the Republic of Korea; Myanmar; Malaysia; the Philippines; Singapore; Thailand; and Viet Nam) have already been operating DVP model 1 with RTGS function. The Lao PDR is developing CSD systems with DVP model 1, while Cambodia is planning to develop a CSD system with DVP model 1.

Regarding corporate bond markets, nine economies (the PRC; Hong Kong, China; Indonesia; Japan; the Republic of Korea; Malaysia; the Philippines; Singapore; and Thailand) are operating DVP model 1 with RTGS function. Five economies (Brunei Darussalam, Cambodia, the Lao PDR, Myanmar, and Viet Nam) are planning to develop CSD systems with DVP model 1.

Real-time processing is a very important issue for high-value payment and settlement systems (HVPS). Compared with Europe and the US, some economies in ASEAN+3 have higher real-time processing capability, such as notifying settlement results including debit and credit as well as the balance of accounts immediately after the settlement. To follow best practices in the region, it is advisable that the customer debit–credit notification (i.e., camt.054 under ISO) include the balance information on a real-time basis to notify both the debit and credit side immediately. A possible change request for camt.054 is shown in Appendix 3 for future discussion.

## 3.    Blocking securities

For government bond markets, 10 economies (Brunei Darussalam; the PRC; Hong Kong, China; Indonesia; the Republic of Korea; Malaysia; the Philippines; Singapore; Thailand; and Viet Nam) have already implemented blocking securities for DVP settlement, whereas the CSD systems in two economies (Japan and Myanmar) do not have such a function. However, Japan is developing this feature. Meanwhile, two economies (Cambodia and the Lao PDR) need to develop their respective CSD systems.

Regarding corporate bonds, 10 economies (the PRC; Hong Kong, China; Indonesia; Japan; the Republic of Korea; Malaysia; the Philippines; Singapore; Thailand; and Viet Nam) have already implemented a block securities function. Four economies (Brunei Darussalam; Cambodia; the Lao PDR; and Myanmar) are required to develop a CSD system with a block securities function for each economy to implement the cross-border DVP.

## 4. Matching

For government bond markets, 11 economies (Brunei Darussalam; the PRC; Hong Kong, China; Indonesia; Japan; the Republic of Korea; Malaysia; the Philippines; Singapore; Thailand; and Viet Nam) have adopted central matching, which confirms both the sell and buy sides' intention to settle. Regarding corporate bond markets, most CSD systems operating in the region have adopted central matching, except for Brunei Darussalam.

## 5. Operating hours

Regarding operating hours, including cut-off times for the business operation of cross-currency DVP, all ASEAN+3 members have indicated that their RTGS and CSD systems have sufficiently overlapping operating hours. However, there are differences in individual markets' schedules such as the start time of DVP processing, cut-off times for different events, and the end of DVP processing each day. Therefore, operating hours for cross-currency DVP should be decided bilaterally. Also, when actual linkages involve more than two economies, operating hours should be discussed among ASEAN+3 members.

## 6. Business continuity planning

Contingency measures based on those outlined in Principles for Financial Market Infrastructures have, in principle, been accepted by all ASEAN+3 member economies. When actual linkages are established, more detailed contingency measures need to be determined. Therefore, BCP issues also need to be revisited after actual linkages have been established so that market participants agree upon the standard or minimum measures to be implemented.

# V. EMERGING TRENDS IN CROSS-BORDER TRANSACTIONS

## A. Cross-Border Collateral

As economic and financial linkages within ASEAN+3 are increasing, collateral demands for cross-border transactions and the need for LCY liquidity will increase. Therefore, CSIF members studied and discussed the possibility of using collateral in one economy to obtain liquidity in another, which is referred to as cross-border collateral.

### 1. Cross-border use of collateral in the Eurosystem

Cross-border collateral transactions are commonly used in the euro area.[11] A bank in country A can get local liquidity from the central bank in country A (home central bank) or another bank in country A by pledging bonds in country C through the correspondent central banking model. This model not only facilitates access to liquidity for banks that are operating across the euro area, but it also increases liquidity in the government bond market (Figure 14).

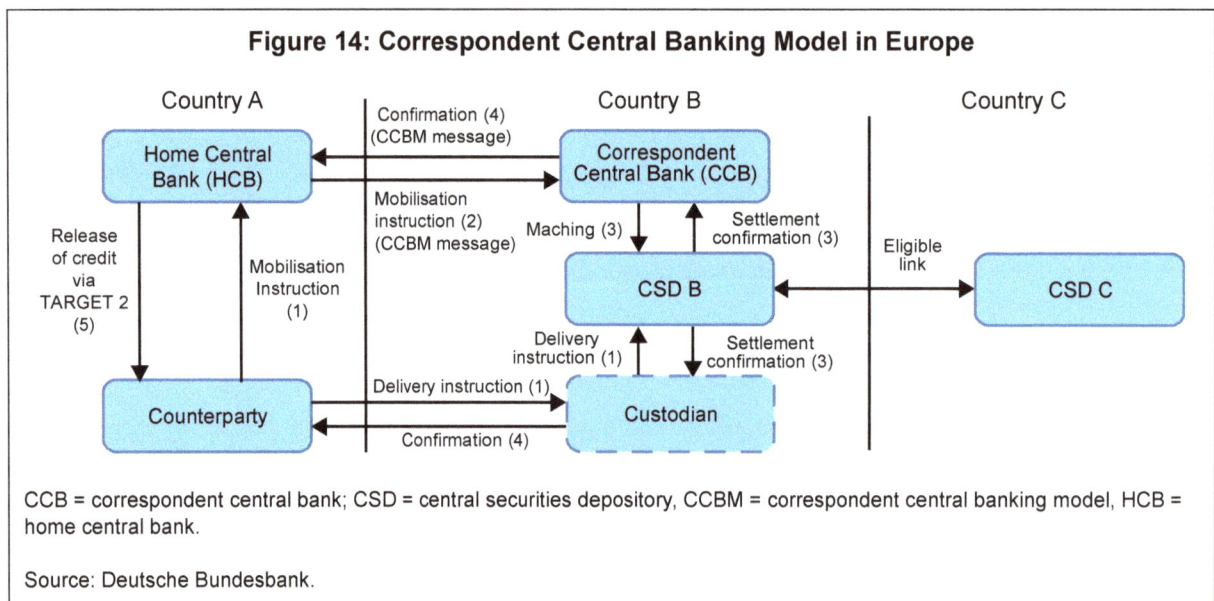

**Figure 14: Correspondent Central Banking Model in Europe**

CCB = correspondent central bank; CSD = central securities depository, CCBM = correspondent central banking model, HCB = home central bank.

Source: Deutsche Bundesbank.

---

[11] Bank for International Settlements. 2006. *Cross-Border Collateral Arrangements*. Basel.

In Europe, the enhancement and connection of region-wide payment and settlement systems were conducted together with the introduction of the euro. First, HVPS or RTGS systems in the euro area were connected with each other via the Trans-European Automated Real-Time Gross Settlement Express Transfer System (TARGET) Interlinking System. Then, the TARGET Interlinking System was consolidated into a single shared platform called TARGET 2. For securities settlement, TARGET 2 Securities was developed with the auto-collateralization mechanism. Furthermore, an initiative to consolidate TARGET 2 and TARGET 2 Securities into a single platform is underway (Figure 15). Such enhancements of payment and settlement infrastructures is expected to contribute to the further development of financial markets in Europe.

**Figure 15: Eurosystem Collateral Management System as Part of Vision 2020**

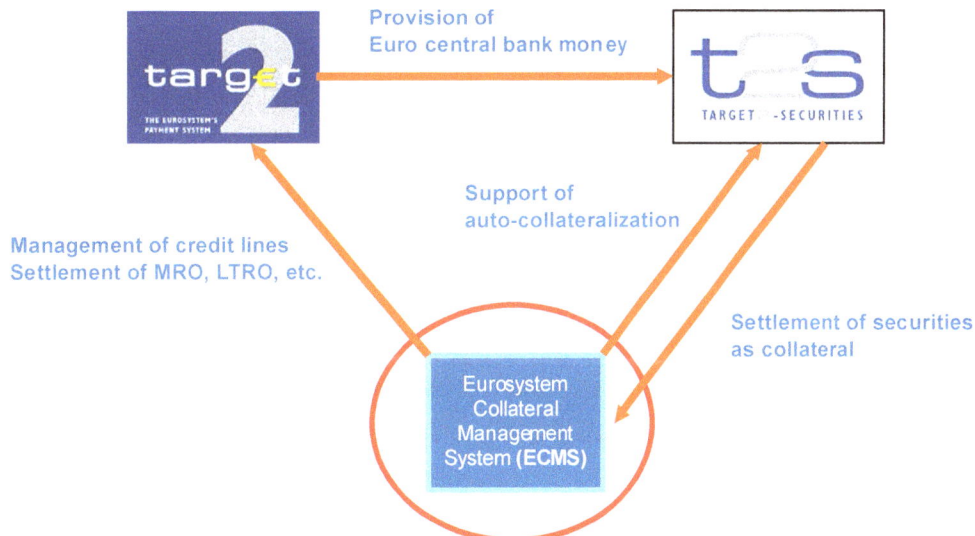

ECMS = Eurosystem Collateral Management System, MRO = main refinancing operation, LTRO = longer-term refinancing operation.

Source: Deutsche Bundesbank.

## 2. Cross-border collateral services by China Central Depository & Clearing Co., Ltd.

With respect to the currency swap transaction between commercial banks in the PRC and foreign central banks, Chinese banks accept CNY-denominated bonds held by the foreign central banks as collateral to control the credit risk from their counterparties to ensure that the swap contract can be successfully implemented (Figure 16).

**Figure 16: Currency Swap Between Banks in the People's Republic of China and Foreign Central Banks**

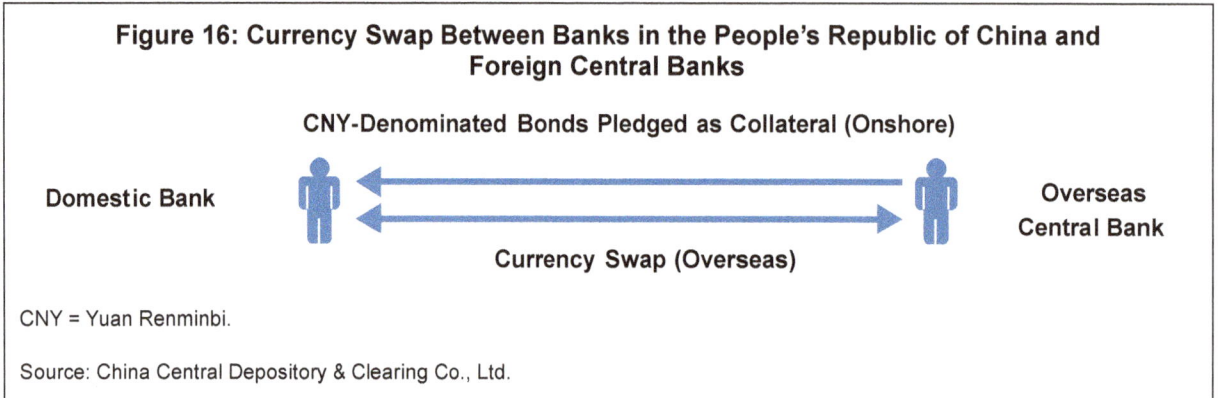

CNY = Yuan Renminbi.

Source: China Central Depository & Clearing Co., Ltd.

## 3. Korea Securities Depository's foreign-currency-denominated customer repo service

Korea Securities Depository has been operating the tri-party repo services since 1999. In December 2018, responding to customer and marketplace demands, Korea Securities Depository introduced a foreign currency-denominated customer repo service to (i) increase market liquidity by utilizing offshore securities as repo collaterals, (ii) reinforce investor protections with increased transparency, and (iii) improve the effectiveness of market monitoring by financial authorities (Figure 17).

**Figure 17: Foreign Currency-Denominated Repo Service**

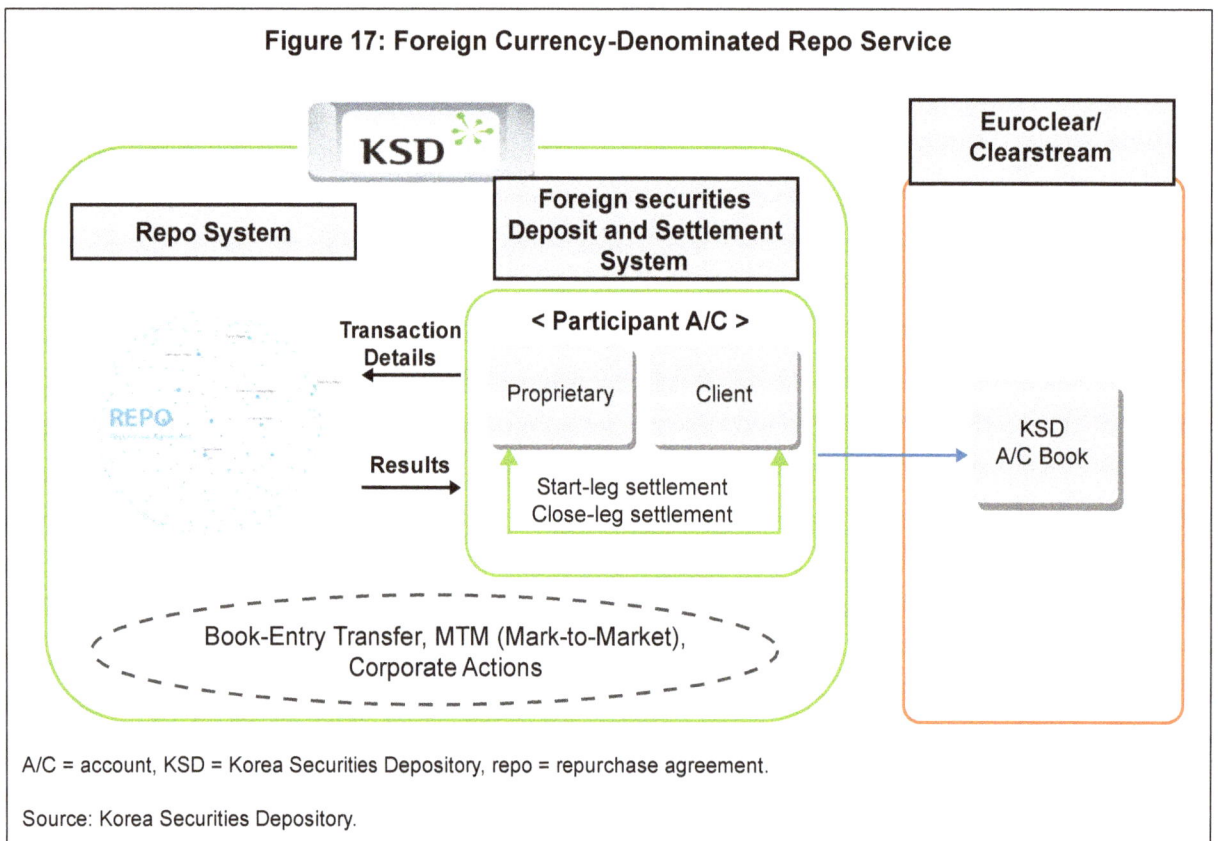

A/C = account, KSD = Korea Securities Depository, repo = repurchase agreement.

Source: Korea Securities Depository.

## 4.  Regional collateral pool

The Asian Prime Collateral Forum shared its proposal to expand the eligibility of central bank collateral within ASEAN+3. As a general practice, a central bank's collateral is restricted to domestic assets such as the government bonds under its jurisdiction. If central banks in the region agreed to expand eligibility to include the government and other qualified bonds of ASEAN+3 member economies, whether via bilateral or multilateral collateral arrangements, it would increase cross-border bond transactions, thereby improving market liquidity and enhancing financial stability in ASEAN+3 markets.

In October 2019, the Asian Prime Collateral Forum jointly organized a session at the 19th CSIF Meeting to discuss the respective collateral frameworks of ASEAN+3 central banks and to explore the possible expansion of the collateral pool for cross-border transactions. More than 100 people, including researchers and government officials in the region, participated in the session and shared their ideas of expanding the collateral pool in ASEAN+3. The discussions enhanced participants' understanding of the segmented collateral and repo markets in the region, allowing them to envision a practical roadmap toward more harmonized transactions. Expanding cross-border collateral arrangements among the region's central banks, together with currency swaps, will help ASEAN+3 protect itself against external shocks and secure the momentum needed to develop the region's LCY bond markets.

## B.    Distributed Ledger Technology

Central banks in the world are conducting various studies, experiments, and assessments of new technologies such as distributed ledger technology (DLT) and blockchain. Some central banks in ASEAN+3 have made steps to implement such technologies into their payment and settlement applications.

## 1.  DLT Scripless Bond in Thailand

The Bank of Thailand and the Thailand Securities Depository have launched an initiative, known as DLT Scripless Bond, that adopts DLT and blockchain. The main purpose of the project is to reduce the time from issuance to subsequent settlement of Thai retail government bonds from 15 days to 2 days (T+2). Along with the Bank of Thailand and the Thailand Securities Depository, major Thai banks are also participating in the project. In the system, the selling agent keeps a record of their own customers as distributed ledgers, while the Bank of Thailand and the Thailand Securities Depository keep the master ledger. The process of securities account opening is conducted automatically with smart contracts, and all transactions are time-stamped and lodged in ledgers retained by authorized participants. Thanks to blockchain technology, the recorded information will be immutable (Figure 18).

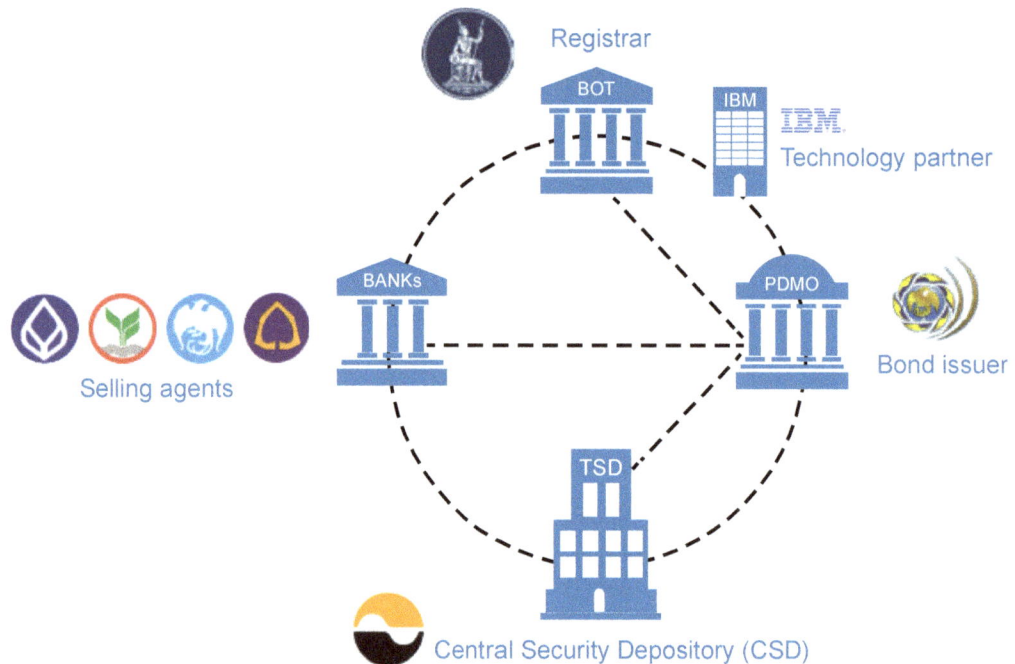

**Figure 18: Distributed Ledger Technology Scripless Bond**

BOT = Bank of Thailand, PDMO = public debt management office, TSD = Thailand Securities Depository Co., Ltd.

Source: Bank of Thailand. 2018. *PROJECT DLT Scripless Bond*. Bangkok.

## 2.  The Bakong System in Cambodia

The Bakong System is a blockchain-based payment service supported by National Bank of Cambodia. It can provide a peer-to-peer fund transfer service to retail customers of participating banks in Cambodia. The service is provided through a mobile app that enables the transfer of funds across the platform on a continuous basis by using a personalized QR code or mobile phone number, instead of a bank account number. To register, a customer needs to have a national identification card or passport and local valid phone number. The Bakong System will connect financial institutions and payment service providers and serve as the backbone for real-time retail payment in Cambodia (Figure 19).

**Figure 19: Bakong System in Cambodia**

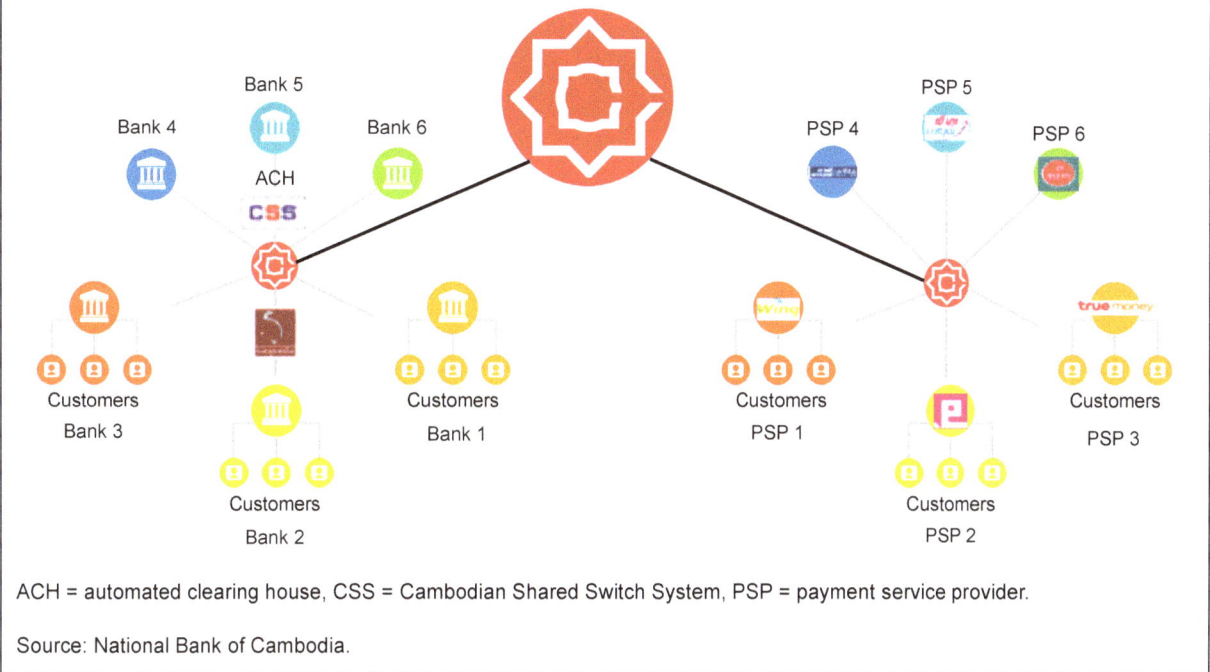

ACH = automated clearing house, CSS = Cambodian Shared Switch System, PSP = payment service provider.

Source: National Bank of Cambodia.

# VI. FUTURE CHALLENGES AND NEXT STEPS

## A. Future Challenges

Establishing an RSI is an effective way to stimulate intraregional financial investments. The CSIF has made concerted efforts toward establishing secure, stable, and efficient cross-border funds and securities settlement infrastructure through CSD–RTGS linkages. The CSIF publications on this subject are the outcome of such efforts. Since the level of market developments among ASEAN+3 economies is diverse, it is necessary to consider measures to support market development in the region's less-developed economies. Proposed measures should provide guidance on supporting market development and furthering market integration to maximize the benefits of regional cooperation. To successfully implement an RSI, the following issues require further attention from CSIF members.

### 1. Cross-border business continuity planning and cybersecurity

While the CSIF has already published the Common Understanding on Cross-Border Business Continuity Planning and Cybersecurity, it is necessary to continuously review these important issues. The process of information sharing and discussion among CSIF members will help crystalize the region's expectation for BCP, cybersecurity standards, system security, and system resiliency. The exchange of information and communication will establish the basis of mutual assurance and recognition needed for systems to be linked in the future.

### 2. Expansion of data exchanges through financial market infrastructure

Thanks to the efforts of CSIF members, all ASEAN+3 markets will soon implement ISO 20022. To maximize the benefits of ISO 20022, the expansion of data fields for cross-border messaging and the possible benefits of data exchanges through market infrastructure should be considered. For example, the European Securities and Markets Authority, the European Union's securities markets regulator, sets ISO 20022 XML schemas to be used for reporting under the Securities Financing Transactions Regulation. Likewise, regulators in ASEAN+3 can consider a standardized regulatory reporting format to maximize the use of XML. Thanks to the use of XML in ISO 20022, Asian local language characters may be accommodated in the future. Currently, cross-border messages are only alphanumeric. To improve know-your-customer processes, ensure anti-money laundering, and combat the financing of terrorism, it is desirable to accept local language characters in the identification of counterparties and monitoring of financial transactions. Such regional efforts should be incorporated into global standards and practices. These issues can be discussed within the ASEAN+3 Bond Market Forum.

## 3.   Rapid technological advancement

Recent technological advancements are supporting the region's market development. Less-developed markets can more easily catch up with or even surpass developed markets because of such rapid advances. The cost of servers has been slashed, and affordable cloud sourcing has made easier the setting up of backup facilities. The expansion of mobile technology is supporting access to information, the digitalization of financial transactions, and the personalization of information that can support faster and more robust identification. The use of QR codes is proliferating in the region, and faster and instantaneous payments are now more widely available in different markets. In addition, the border of wholesale and retail payments is blurring as some central banks are supporting such payments through the central bank system. The existing cross-border banking network based on correspondent agreements between banks is facing challenges as new technologies support the establishment of secured and traceable cross-border payment networks. Given the heightened risk of cybersecurity, an existing framework of network security can quickly become obsolete. In previous CSIF discussions, it was assumed that further development of CSD–RTGS linkages between all members would require a centralized unit to facilitate smooth cross-border data exchanges and transactions. However, it is not clear such an assumption still holds. In the current technological environment, the most suitable system architecture for the region needs to take such advancements into account. Therefore, the CSIF may need to conduct more research on available technologies such as DLT, blockchain, and tokenization.

## 4.   Linkages between securities and cash payment system

As described in previous sections, CSD–RTGS linkages will support not only securities settlement but also cross-border PVP. Given the increase in intraregional transactions amid remaining frictions in cross-border currency transactions, it is necessary to consider how CSD–RTGS linkages can support cross-currency liquidity provision. Without an actual cash fund transfer, the pledging of high-quality liquid local currency assets could supplement and support local currency payments. Since most ASEAN+3 markets operate in either the same (or an adjacent) time zone, regional CSD–RTGS linkages would create additional market liquidity.

## B.    Next Steps

Rapidly proliferating disruptive technologies such as DLT, blockchain, crypto-asset, and tokenization could substantially influence the future technical architecture of payment and settlement systems in the region, including CSD–RTGS linkages. Therefore, the CSIF should study the possible impacts of such technologies thoroughly. Some central banks in the region have already announced the extensive study and assessment of central bank digital currencies, while other central banks in the region have already implemented such technologies. Given the uncertainty surrounding certain new technologies, further studies and analyses are needed. As some economies in ASEAN+3 are more advanced in the utilization of such technologies, important leading cases can be observed. By exchanging information among CSIF members, knowledge and experiences can be shared. Given the possible impact on cross-border payment and settlement systems, the CSIF may need to consider further technical specifications and operational implementation of CSD–RTGS linkages in the evolving technological environment.

To create more concrete opportunities for cross-border transactions, the collateral usage of government bonds for LCY-to-LCY cross-border transactions and liquidity management needs to be discussed and studied continuously and in depth. Enriched regional collateral pools for cross-border monetary transactions are another important component of the regional safety net.

The cross-border DVP linkage between the Bank of Japan and the HKMA, which is expected to go live in spring 2021, is a leading example and an important benchmark case for further implementation in other jurisdictions across the region. Therefore, the CSIF should support the successful launching of this and other similar initiatives involving members of ASEAN+3.

## Appendix 1: Members, Observers, and Secretariat including Liaison Persons

**1. Members including participants and liaison persons from member institutions**

### BRUNEI DARUSSALAM (BN)

#### Autoriti Monetari Brunei Darussalam (AMBD)

Mardini bin Hj Eddie, Monetary Operations/International & Development

Dk Hjh Faadzilah PDP Hj Abu Bakar, Capital Market, Regulatory and Supervision

Ak Mohd Mas Nazirul Hasheer Pg Hj Masuni, Capital Market, Regulatory and Supervision

Syafiiqah Aamirah Awg Mohd Abdoh, Capital Market, Regulatory and Supervision

Lim Shaw Fhen, Payment & Settlement System

Siti Naasirah Hj Mohd Mahdi, Payment & Settlement System

Ak Muhammad Hafizuddin Bin Pg Hassanuddin, Payment & Settlement System

Dyg Siti Aimi Awg Matali, Payment & Settlement System

Hjh Mahani Binti Hj Mohsin, International

Shifa' Binti Husaini, International

### CAMBODIA (KH)

#### National Bank of Cambodia (NBC)

Ouk Sarat, Payment System Department

Kho Virada, Payment System Department

#### Cambodia Securities Exchange (CSX)

Chanmony Sou, Securities Depository Department

Taihy Try, Securities Clearing and Settlement Department

### PEOPLE'S REPUBLIC OF CHINA (CN)

#### The People's Bank of China (PBOC)

Wu Tong, Payment and Settlement Department

Cheng Shigang, Payment and Settlement Department

Xue Chen, Payment and Settlement Department

Yin Shi, Payment and Settlement Department

Chen Song, International Department

Lyu Yuan, Payment and Settlement Department

Huang Jing, Payment and Settlement Department

Zeyang Yu, Payment and Settlement Department

Wang Changxin, International Department

Jing Rong, Shenzhen Branch Cross-border RMB Business Pilot Office (Cross-Border Office)

## China Central Depository & Clearing Co., Ltd. (CCDC)

Yahua Ding, Technical Planning Department

Huiming Wang, New Generation System Development Department

Yitao Xu, New Generation System Development Department

Huayun Tang, CCDC Development and Testing Center

Shengnan Guo, Cross-border Settlement Center

Hongqiang Gu, International Business Department

Xiangyu Zheng, Statistics Department

Chaoqun Wang, China Bond Pricing Center

Lei Ma, China Bond Enterprise Bond Assessment Center

Minjie Tan, Issuance Department

Jiheng Zhao, Application Development Department

Yang Bai, Cross-border Settlement Center

Hao Geng, Operation and Maintenance Center

Bingqing Ma, Development and Testing Center

Yini Wang, Cross-border Settlement Center

Shixuan Gao, China Bond Pricing Center

Tianhui Gao, CCDC Collateral Management Service Center

Peng Wang, Depository Department

Yan Jia, Cash Settlement

Chen Li, Technical Planning Department

Jing Luo, Innovation & Research, Depository Department

Yulu  Pu, China Bond Collateral Management Center, Shanghai HQ

Fei Tao, Collateral Management Service Center, Shanghai HQ

Ping Jiang, Cross-border Settlement Center, Shanghai HQ

Jun Zong, Innovation Department, CCDC Shenzhen

Liyuan Zhu, Bond Department, CCDC Shenzhen

Yushan Li, Issuance Department, CCDC Shenzhen

Haitao Yao, Customer Service Department, CCDC Shenzhen


## China Securities Depository & Clearing Corporation., Ltd. (CSDC)

Liyuan Zhu, Bond Business Department

Xiaolei He, Risk Monitoring Department

Jing Xu, Bond Business Department

Cheng Xu, Bond Business Department

Yang  Liu, Bond Business Department

Haoda Liu, Risk Monitoring Department

Yun Zhu, Shanghai Branch, Business Development Department

Rui Wang, Shanghai Branch, Issuer Service Department

Bo Zhou, Shenzhen Branch, Risk Monitoring Department

Wenlin Liao, Shenzhen Branch, Issuer Service Department

Qingtao Guan, Shenzhen Branch, Settlement Department

Zishan Tan, Shenzhen Branch, Settlement Department

### Shanghai Clearing House (SHCH)

Bingqing Xie, Issuance and Custody Department

Ye Tao, Issuance and Custody Department

## HONG KONG, CHINA (HK)

### Hong Kong Monetary Authority (HKMA)

Yuk Kuen Ng, Financial Infrastructure Development

Hiu Fung Tse, Financial Infrastructure Development

Kwok Hung Lee, Financial Infrastructure Development

## INDONESIA (ID)

### Bank Indonesia (BI)

Evy Rita Berliana, Payment System Management Department

Siti Hidayati, Payment System Policy Department

Anton Daryono, Financial System Surveillance Department

Aloysius Donanto, National Payment Gateway and Electronification Department

Jultarda Hutagalung, Payment System Management Department

Aida Fitri, Payment System Policy Department

Devi Riyanti, Payment System Management Department

Ngadino, Payment System Management Department

Putu Paulus Adi S., Payment System Policy Department

Nesa Deskandini, Payment System Management Department

### PT Kustodian Sentral Efek Indonesia (KSEI) / Indonesia Central Securities Depository

Racmi Maryda Ramyakim, Corporate Secretary, Project Management and Risk Management Division

Aditya Kresna Priambudi, Strategic Planning Unit

## JAPAN (JP)

### Bank of Japan (BOJ)

Mayuko Miki

Hideto Sakashita

### Japan Securities Depository Center, Inc. (JASDEC)

Tanaka Koji, Corporate Strategy Department

Sato Yuji, Corporate Strategy Department

Saika Tatsuhiko, Corporate Strategy Department

## REPUBLIC OF KOREA (KR)

### Bank of Korea (BOK)

Junhong Park, Payment and Settlement Systems Department

Hyein Jin, Payment and Settlement Systems Department

Hyung Koo Lee, Payment and Settlement Systems Department

Nayeon Park, Payment and Settlement Systems Department

Kiju Yeom, Payment and Settlement Systems Department

Youngseok Kim, Payment and Settlement Systems Department

Jisung Ko, Payment and Settlement Systems Department

Sooyeon Choi, Payment and Settlement Systems Department

Leelark Park, Payment and Settlement Systems Department

Byoung Mok Lee, Payment and Settlement Systems Department

Wonsik Jung, International Affairs Department

Taekjeong Nam, Payment and Settlement Systems Department

Dongjae Lee, International Affairs Department

### Korea Securities Depository (KSD)

Seungkwon Lee, Global Business Department

Jeonghyun Noh, Global Business Department

Mi Sun Park, Clearing & Settlement Department

Minsoo Kim, Global Business Department

Taeyun Kim, Clearing & Settlement Department

## LAO PEOPLE'S DEMOCRATIC REPUBLIC (LA)

### Bank of the Lao PDR (BOL)

Soulysak Thamnuvong, Payment Systems Department

Lammone Simmalaivong, Payment Systems Department

Viengdaly Souphanouvong, Lao Securities Commission Office

Nakhonsy Manodham, Lao Securities Commission Office

Latsamy Souvanthong, Information Technology Department

Phoutsala Omdala, Information Technology Department

Sengthavong Luanglath, Information Technology Department

Phetvilay Vannabouathong, Lao Securities Commission Office

## MALAYSIA (MY)

### Bank Negara Malaysia (BNM)

Yip Kah Kit, Financial Development and Innovation

Safiyyah Mohsin, Financial Development and Innovation

Daniel Khaw, Financial Development and Innovation

## MYANMAR (MM)

### Central Bank of Myanmar (CBM)

Su Su Nwe, Financial Market Department (Accounts Department)

Ni Lar Swe, Financial Market Department (Accounts Department)

Aye Mya Nyein, Financial Market Department (Accounts Department)

## PHILIPPINES (PH)

### Bangko Sentral ng Pilipinas (BSP)

Eleanor Turaray, Payments and Settlements Office

### Bureau of the Treasury (BTr)

Rosalia De Leon, Office of the Treasurer of the Philippines

Erwin Sta. Ana, Office of the Deputy Treasurer of the Philippines

Ma. Nanette Diaz, Office of the Director for Liability Management Service

Arturo II Trinidad, Liability Management Service

Claire Kismet Diaz, Liability Management Service

Michael Laurence Dizon, Liability Management Service

### Philippine Dealing System Group (PDS Group) / Philippine Depository & Trust Corporation (PDTC)

Ma. Theresa Ravalo, President

Sheila Ramos, Asset Services/Corporate Action

## SINGAPORE (SG)

### Singapore Exchange (SGX) / Central Depository (CDP)

Nico Torchetti, Post Trade Services

Lum Yong Teng, Depository Operations

## THAILAND (TH)

### Bank of Thailand (BOT)

Wasna Nimityongskul, Payment and Bond Department

Pensiri Wangdan, Payment and Bond Department

Wipat Wattanasiriwiroj, Payment and Bond Department

Sirirat Junwongsasin, Payment and Bond Department

Worachai Chiamchittrong Payment and Bond Department

Kantitat Areechitranusorn, Payment and Bond Department

Daungporn Rodpengsangkaha, International Department

Jittapa Prachuabmoh, International Department

Sasinan Pantuna, Payment Systems Policy Department

### Thailand Securities Depository Co., Ltd. (TSD)

Pataravasee Suvarnsorn, Senior Executive Vice President, Head of Market Operations Division

Yupawan Sirichainarumitr, Managing Director

Lucksana Tungtulakorn, Depository Department

Yukolthorn Sakdasathaporn, Post Trade Business Development Department

Pornpreeya Vatthanasuk, Depository Department

Nattawan Jiranakorn, Post Trade Business Development Department

## VIET NAM (VN)

### State Bank of Vietnam (SBV)

Van Duc Ngo, Payment Department

Phu Thai Dung Nguyen, IT Department

Thi Hoa Nguyen, International Cooperation Department

### Vietnam Securities Depository (VSD)

Dung Luu Trung, R&D and International Co-operation Division

## 2.  Observers including liaison persons

### ASEAN SECRETARIAT

Ho Quang Trung, ASEAN Economic Community Department

Jonathan Panggabean, ASEAN Economic Community Department

## CAMBODIA (KH)

### Ministry of Economy and Finance (MEF)

Chou Vannak, General Department of Financial Industry

Ney Sakal, General Department of Financial Industry

No Lida, General Department of Financial Industry

Buth Vanny, General Department of Financial Industry

Kuth Daravichhay, General Department of Financial Industry

Vong Senpiseth, General Department of Financial Industry

Po Seanghan, General Department of Financial Industry

### Security and Exchange Commission of Cambodia (SECC)

Socheat Sou, Director General

Dara Sok, Deputy Director General

Sambath Chhun, Deputy Director General

Rady Mok, Research, Training, Securities Market Development and International Relations

Channa Lim, Securities Issuance

Pochkhy Khy, Research, Training, Securities Market Development and International Relations

Veasna Khun, Research, Training, Securities Market Development and International Relations

Piseth Sok, Securities Market Supervision

Rortana Chreng, Securities Issuance

Ratha Rin, Securities Intermediaries Supervision

Vannet Siv, Securities Market Supervision

Samul Heng, Research, Training, Securities Market Development and International Relations

Soklin Seng, Research, Training, Securities Market Development and International Relations

Panha Kuy, Securities Market Supervision

## PEOPLE'S REPUBLIC OF CHINA (CN)

### Ministry of Finance

Zhengwei Zhang, Department of International Economic Relations

Feng Gong, Department of International Economic Relations

Qi Zhang, Department of International Economic Relations

Yuan Tian, Department of International Economic Relations

Mengli Wu, Department of International Economic Relations

## INDONESIA (ID)

### Ministry of Finance

Dian Lestari, Center for Regional and Bilateral Policy

Vincentius Krisna Juli Wicaksono, Center for Regional and Bilateral Policy

Sepriza Triasanditya, Center for Regional and Bilateral Policy

Evan Oktavianus, Center for Regional and Bilateral Policy

Titis Ayu Putranto, Center for Regional and Bilateral Policy

Yudha Perdana, Center for Regional and Bilateral Policy

### Otoritas Jasa Keuangan (OJK) / Financial Services Authority (FSA)

Agustyatun Muji Rahayu Prihatin, Department of Capital Market Supervision 2A

## JAPAN (JP)

### Ministry of Finance Japan

Mina   Kajiyama, International Bureau

Kazuma Komori, International Bureau

Akira Tokunaga, International Bureau

Takeshi Koike, International Bureau

Tatsuya Sato, International Bureau

Yuto Okuhata, International Bureau

## REPUBLIC OF KOREA (KR)

### Ministry of Economy and Finance

Dong-Ick Kim, International Finance Bureau

Eunkyoung Choi, International Finance Bureau

Jeong-a Lee, International Finance Bureau

Younghwan Ahn, International Finance Bureau

Taekmin Lee, International Finance Bureau

## LAO PEOPLE'S DEMOCRATIC REPUBLIC (LA)

### Ministry of Finance

Vanida Savaddy, External Finance and Debt Management

Sengaloun Inmyxai, External Finance and Debt Management

## MALAYSIA (MY)

### Ministry of Finance

Zarina Zakaria, International Division

Nor Hazlina Ab Aziz, International Division

Norhaslinda Mohd Sibi, International Division

Nur Amalia Anuar, International Division

## MYANMAR (MM)

### Ministry of Planning, Finance and Industry

Ei Sein Sein Kywe, Office of the Securities and Exchange Commission of Myanmar, Development and Policy Department

## PHILIPPINES (PH)

### Department of Finance (DOF)

Mark Dennis Joven, International Finance Group

Maria Edita Z. Tan, International Finance Group

Neil Adrian Cabiles, International Finance Group

Ferdinand Ortilla, International Finance Group

Cindy Nuguit, International Finance Group

### Securities and Exchange Commission (SEC)

Ephyro Luis Barrios Amatong, Office of the Commissioners

Vicente Graciano T. Felizmenio, Jr, Markets and Securities Regulation Department

Emma Valencia, Markets and Securities Regulation Department

Erwin Edward Mendinueto, Markets and Securities Regulation Department

Allysa Ayochok, Markets and Securities Regulation Department

Krizia Pauline Felice Ferrer, Markets and Securities Regulation Department

Jessa Farra Patilleros, Markets and Securities Regulation Department

Rosamund Faye Melig, Markets & Securities Regulation Department

## 3.  Secretariat team

### Asian Development Bank (ADB)

Satoru Yamadera, Economic Research and Regional Cooperation Department

Kosintr Puongsophol, Economic Research and Regional Cooperation Department

Byung-Wook Ahn, Economic Research and Regional Cooperation Department

Taiji Inui, Economic Research and Regional Cooperation Department / *Chief Advisor, CBM TC Project, JICA*

Jae-Hyun, Economic Research and Regional Cooperation Department

Yvonne Osonia, Economic Research and Regional Cooperation Department

# Appendix 2: Basic Requirements for Network Providers of Central Securities Depository–Real-Time Gross Settlement Linkages

1. The network providers should provide services with a high level of security, reliability, and availability (Figure A2).
2. The network providers should have secure user identification, authentication, and authorization scheme and services.
3. The network providers should have a sufficient level of technological capability to support Central Securities Depository–Real-Time Gross Settlement linkages.
4. The network providers should be compliant with the international standards, in particular ISO 20022.
5. The network providers should have a stable management foundation.
6. The network providers should have a switching hub in the ASEAN+3 region.
7. The messages transferred between ASEAN+3 FMIs through the network providers should be processed within the ASEAN+3 region.
8. The backup site of the network hub should also be located in ASEAN+3, but in a different economy than that of the primary site.
9. The network providers should accept cooperative oversight by ASEAN+3 central banks.
10. The network providers should have reasonable cost efficiency and transparency.
11. The network providers should commit to FMIs in ASEAN+3 to provide a sufficient level of services, which will enable FMI operators to provide high-quality services to their participants.

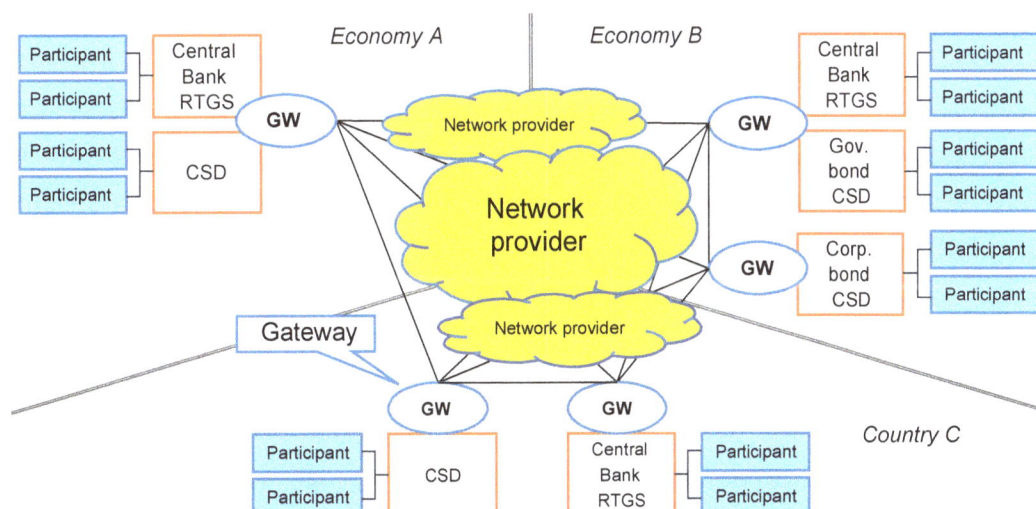

**Figure A2: Network Providers for Central Securities Depository–Real-Time Gross Settlement Linkages**

CSD = central securities depository, GW = gateway, RTGS = real-time gross settlement.

Source: Cross-Border Settlement Infrastructure Forum illustration.

## Appendix 3: Change Request for the Update of ISO 20022

### FINANCIAL REPOSITORY ITEMS (PRELIMINARY DRAFT)

**A.  Origin of the request: Adding Balance to camt.054**

*A.1 Submitter:* Cross-border Settlement Infrastructure Forum (CSIF)

*A.2 Contact person(s):* XXX

**B.  Related messages:**

camt.052.001.08 - BankToCustomerAccountReportV08

camt.054.001.08 - BankToCustomerDebitCreditNotificationV08

**C.  Description of the change request:**

Adding Balance <bal> to camt.054 Debtor Agent and Creditor Agent under RelatedParties <RltdPties>.

RelatedParties is located under the "Notification <Ntfctn> of camt.052.001.08"

"BankToCustomerAccountReportV08" as follows:

4.4.2 Notification <Ntfctn>

4.4.2.14 Entry <Ntry>

4.4.2.14.18 EntryDetails <NtryDtls>

6.1.9.3.2 TransactionDetails<TxDtls>

6.1.9.2.9 RelatedParties <RltdPties>

6.1.9.2.9.2 Debtor <Dbtr>

6.1.9.2.9.5 Creditor <Cdtr>

6.1.21.3.2 Agent <Agt>

6.1.15.4.1 FinancialInstitutionIdentification <FinInstnId>

The Balance <bal> is added under the  Agent <Agt>  as the balance of "6.1.15.4.1 FinancialInstitutionIdentification <FinInstnId>"  as follows:

| No. | Logical Item Name | <XML Tag> | Or | Mult. |
|---|---|---|---|---|
| 1 | + + + + + + + + RelatedParties | <RltdPties> | - | [0..1] |
| 2 | + + + + + + + + + Debtor | <Dbtr> | - | [0..1] |
| 3 | + + + + + + + + + + Party | <Pty> | {Or | [1..1] |
| 4 | + + + + + + + + + + Agent | <Agt> | Or} | [1..1] |
| 5 | + + + + + + + + + + + FinancialInstitutionIdentification | <FinInstnId> | - | [1..1] |
| 6 | + + + + + + + + + + + BICFI | <BICFI> | - | [0..1] |
| 7 | + + + + + + + + + + + Balance | <Bal> | - | [0..1] |
| 8 | + + + + + + + + + + + + Type | <Tp> | - | [1..1] |
| 9 | + + + + + + + + + + + + CreditLine | <CdtLine> | - | [0..1] |
| 10 | + + + + + + + + + + + + Amount | <Amt> | - | [1..1] |
| 11 | + + + + + + + + + + + + CreditDebitIndicator | <CdtDbtInd> | - | [1..1] |
| 12 | + + + + + + + + + + + + Date | <Dt> | - | [1..1] |
| 13 | + + + + + + + + + Creditor | <Cdtr> | - | [0..1] |
| 14 | + + + + + + + + + + Party | <Pty> | {Or | [1..1] |
| 15 | + + + + + + + + + + Agent | <Agt> | Or} | [1..1] |
| 16 | + + + + + + + + + + + FinancialInstitutionIdentification | <FinInstnId> | - | [1..1] |
| 17 | + + + + + + + + + + + BICFI | <BICFI> | - | [0..1] |
| 18 | + + + + + + + + + + + Balance | <Bal> | - | [0..1] |
| 19 | + + + + + + + + + + + + Type | <Tp> | - | [1..1] |
| 20 | + + + + + + + + + + + + CreditLine | <CdtLine> | - | [0..1] |
| 21 | + + + + + + + + + + + + Amount | <Amt> | - | [1..1] |
| 22 | + + + + + + + + + + + + CreditDebitIndicator | <CdtDbtInd> | - | [1..1] |
| 23 | + + + + + + + + + + + + Date | <Dt> | - | [1..1] |

Message items No. 7–12 and No. 18–23 are added to Debtor Agent and Creditor Agent, respectively.

Outline of the message items for the Balance are as follows:

Note: the message items for the Balance are tried to be similar with that for camt.052

**Balance <Bal>**

*Presence:* [0..1]

*Definition:* Set of elements used to define the balance as a numerical representation of the net increases and decreases in an account at a specific point in time.

**Balance <Bal>** contains the following **CashBalance8** elements

Type <Tp> [1..1]

CreditLine <CdtLine> [0..1]

Amount <Amt> [1..1]

CreditDebitIndicator <CdtDbtInd> [1..1]

Date <Dt> [1..1]

*C1. Type <Tp>*

*Presence:* [1..1]

*Definition:* Specifies the nature of a balance.

**Type <Tp>** contains the following elements (see "BalanceType13" for details)

 CodeOrProprietary <CdOrPrtry> [1..1]

　 Code <Cd> [1..1] or Proprietary <Prtry> [1..1]

　SubType <SubTp> [0..1]

　 Code <Cd> [1..1] or Proprietary <Prtry> [1..1]

*C2. CreditLine <CdtLine>*

*Presence:* [0..*]

*Definition:* Set of elements used to provide details on the credit line.

**CreditLine <CdtLine>** contains the following elements (see "CreditLine3" for details)

 Included <Incl> [1..1]

　Type <Tp> [1..1]

　 Code <Cd> [1..1] or Proprietary <Prtry> [1..1]

　Amount <Amt> [0..1]

　Date <Dt> [0..1]

*C3. Amount <Amt>*

*Presence:* [1..1]

*Definition:* Amount of money of the cash balance.

*Impacted by:* C2 "ActiveOrHistoricCurrency", C6 "CurrencyAmount"

*Datatype:* "ActiveOrHistoricCurrencyAndAmount"

　• **ActiveOrHistoricCurrency**

　The Currency Code must be registered, or have already been registered. Valid active or historic currency codes are registered with the ISO 4217 Maintenance Agency, consist of three (3) contiguous letters, and may be or not be withdrawn on the day the message containing the Currency is exchanged.

　• CurrencyAmount

　The number of fractional digits (or minor unit of currency) must comply with ISO 4217.

　Note: The decimal separator is a dot.

*C4. CreditDebitIndicator <CdtDbtInd>*

*Presence:* [1..1]

*Definition:* Indicates whether the balance is a credit or a debit balance.

Usage: A zero balance is considered to be a credit balance.

*Datatype:* "CreditDebitCode"

  CRDT or DBIT


*C5. Date <Dt>*

*Presence:* [1..1]

*Definition:* Indicates the date (and time) of the balance.

**Date <Dt>** contains one of the following elements (see "DateAndDateTime2Choice" for details)

  Date <Dt> or DateTime <DtTm>


## D.  Purpose of the change:

Recently, RTGS is commonly used as the way to settle interbank transactions in particular for HVPS. In such a case, it is important to inform latest balance as the result of the settlement from account servicer to account owners both credit and debit sides.

Generally, camt.054 is used to inform the result of the settlement for HVPS. For this purpose, Balance information is to be added to the Agent under Debtor and Creditor of camt.054, respectively, in order for account servicer to inform the latest balance to account owners in a real-time basis.

Also, the sentence "It does not contain balance information" of "4.1 Message Definition Functionality" will be changed to "It does not contain balance information as mandatory item".


## E.  Urgency of the request:

It is proposed to include this change request in the next regular maintenance cycle.

Some central banks in ASEAN+3 notify balances of current accounts to the participants of RTGS systems immediately after the settlement of each instruction. As such, it is an important request to solve already existing challenges.

➢  In some cases, proprietary message types (and/or items) are used because appropriate credit and debit notification messages in ISO 20022.

## F. Business examples:

An example of HVPS for funds transfers using the central bank RTGS system is shown below. Timely information about the latest balance is important not only for liquidity management of participants (financial institutions) but also for risk management perspective.

### Real-time funds transfer from participant A to participant B
### through a Central Bank (financial market infrastructure) RTGS system

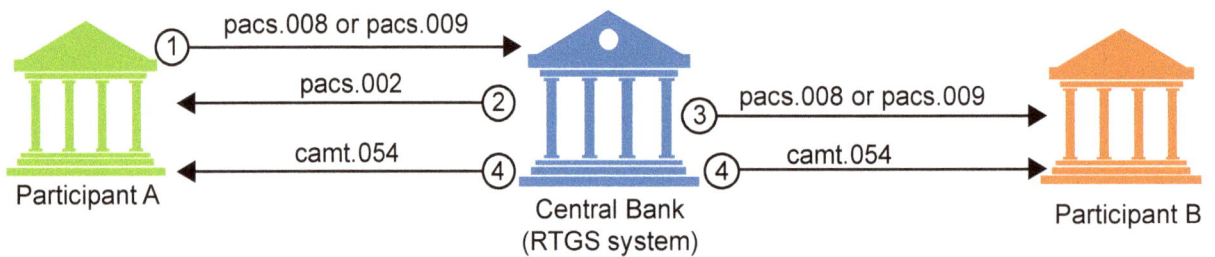

## G. SEG/TSG recommendation:

| Consider | | Timing | | |
|----------|--|--------|--|--|
|  |  |  |  |  |

Comments:

| Reject | |
|--------|--|

Reason for rejection:

# Appendix 4: Terms of Reference of Cross-Border Settlement Infrastructure Forum

**ASEAN+3 Cross-Border Settlement Infrastructure Forum**

## I.  Purpose

In order to produce tangible and concrete outcomes going forward, ASEAN+3 Finance Ministers and Central Bank Governors adopted the New Roadmap+ in May 2012. The New Roadmap+ identifies nine priorities, one of which is facilitating the establishment of the Regional Settlement Intermediary (RSI). The Cross-Border Settlement Infrastructure Forum (the Forum) will be a key instrument to support Task Force 4 (TF4) of the Asian Bond Markets Initiative (ABMI) in facilitating discussion on the improvement of cross-border bond and cash settlement infrastructure in the region including the establishment of RSI.

The Forum aims to

(i)  enhance dialogue among policy makers and operators of bond and cash settlement infrastructure in the region;

(ii)  assess the existing settlement infrastructures and identify comprehensive issues and requirements to facilitate cross-border bond and cash settlement infrastructure in the region;

(iii)  develop common basic principles for cross-border bond and cash settlement infrastructure in medium- and long-term perspective; and

(iv)  discuss prospective models, overall roadmap, and implementation plan for the establishment of cross-border bond and cash settlement infrastructure in the region.

## II.  Function

The Forum shall function as a platform to discuss and collaborate among policy makers and operators in the region in order for improvement of cross-border bond and cash settlement infrastructure to facilitate bonds and cash transactions in the region.

The Forum shall submit a progress report, work plan, and recommendations for the establishment of cross-border bond and cash settlement infrastructure to the ABMI TF4.

## III.    Membership and participants

Membership consists of (i) National Members (policy makers) and (ii) National Members (operators).

- National Members (policy makers): Central Banks responsible for cash settlement and policy makers responsible for corporate and sovereign bonds settlement. Participation of the Central Banks and the policy makers is voluntary.

- National Members (operators): National Central Securities Depositories (NCSDs) responsible for operations of settling corporate and sovereign bonds. National Members (policy makers) shall nominate National Members (operators) of respective economies as appropriate.

- Asian Development Bank (ADB): ADB will serve as the Secretariat.

- Experts:  Experts shall be nominated with consent of other national members, if warranted. Experts shall contribute to discussion related to cross-border bond and cash transaction in the region.

## IV.    Chair

Two co-chairs shall be elected among national members (policy makers). Vice-chairs shall be elected by members in order to support co-chairs as appropriate. Term of chairs shall be 1 year and may be reappointed.